SHIFT to Professional Paradise

5 Steps to Less Stress, More Energy & Remarkable Results at Work

VICKI HESS

SHIFT to
Professional
Paradise

5 Steps to Less Stress,
More Energy &
Remarkable Results at Work

Printed in the United States of America
ISBN: 978-1-4538508-6-2

Credits

Collaborative Editor	Juli Baldwin, The Baldwin Group, Plano, TX Juli@BaldwinGrp.com
Copy Editor	Kathleen Green, Positively Proofed, Plano, TX info@PositivelyProofed.com
Design, art direction, and production	Melissa Monogue, Back Porch Creative, Plano, TX info@BackPorchCreative.com

Contents

Foreword

It's understandable not to love your work.

It's even understandable to hate your work at times.

But comparing your job to a wonderland or Utopia? Looking forward to Monday morning meetings as if they were picnics at the beach? That's pretty far-fetched. In fact, it's quite a stretch for many people.

And yet, it's an intriguing stretch, a tantalizing stretch, and a very desirable one.

According to Vicki Hess, it is a stretch that is certainly worth the effort, and one that is definitely attainable. Having reached the invigorating and inspiring place of "job nirvana" herself, Vicki explains how the rest of us can find the same.

As entertaining as it is enlightening, this book, however, is not for the faint of heart. It doesn't coddle and it doesn't cater. What it does is make us realize that we are the ones responsible for our attitudes toward work. Not the short-tempered boss or the patronizing coworker, but *us*.

That realization, Vicki maintains, is the key to unlocking the "professional prison" we often find ourselves in and the first step in transforming it into a "professional paradise."

But of course, there's more to it than that. There's much more to learn, and Vicki lays out the lesson plans carefully, thoroughly and quite cheerfully so we understand how to change our work environments by persistently changing our outlooks and responses.

What makes this book universal, and not just applicable to the job setting, is that the actions she offers work equally well in any stressful or difficult situation. In short, by following Vicki's advice, any human encounter can become a good one.

An escape artist with Houdini-like confidence and smoothness, Vicki guides us as readers to a new way of thinking, engaging and behaving that will ultimately lead to satisfaction and fulfillment in that necessary, but not always affirming, workplace environment.

Professional paradise actually does exist. Believe me, after reading *SHIFT to Professional Paradise*, you'll agree that what seems like only an imaginary fantasy can truly become a reality.

Simon T. Bailey
CEO, The Brilliance Institute, Inc.
Best-selling author of *Release Your Brilliance: The 4 Steps to Transforming Your Life and Revealing Your Genius to the World* (HarperCollins 2008)

Believe It...or Not

Okay, all you doubting Thomases...let me set your mind at ease: **Professional Paradise** *does* **exist**.

How do I know? I've worked in Professional Paradise for many years. I perpetually experience less stress and more energy and achieve remarkable results at work. I call this "the good life." I put up my umbrella, sit back in a cozy chair, feel the warm breeze on my face, listen to the sounds of the ocean, dig my bare toes in the warm sand of work and experience all that Professional Paradise has to offer.

There's just one problem...

I'm lonely!

While I'm delightfully going about my workday, millions of you are toiling away in Professional Prison. As a professional speaker, I often present in front of large audiences. I see the faces of people who think and act as if they have no control over their lives at work and who blame others for their circumstances. Have you ever noticed that "they" (whoever that might be at the time) do a lot of unfair things to people? *Customers are so demanding. My coworkers make my life miserable. My boss keeps changing his mind!* You've probably heard all these things, and maybe even said them yourself.

In my consulting business, I walk the halls of organizations just like yours. I hear the voices of people who are stuck in the rut of complaining. Did you know that in many offices it's considered "cool" to be cranky? *Why can't that department get its act together? Why should I have to work so hard when no one else does?* How does the grousing and grumbling affect you day-to-day?

I facilitate meetings and training sessions where I experience too much negativity, judgment and closed mindedness. Have you noticed how often people are imprisoned by their own beliefs and opinions, unwilling to see or hear another perspective? *That will never work. They're doing this intentionally to hurt me. That can't be right.* Sound familiar? Isn't it a bit disturbing to you that pessimism rules the day?

All the latest surveys and research support what I see every day: **too many people are not happy at work**. Call it disengagement; call it burned out; call it what you want. I call it *sad*. It's hard to believe that in our privileged society so many people are so disappointed in what they do for a living that stress, depression and disease run rampant in workplaces across America.

I'm sick and tired of seeing bright, talented, exceptional individuals locked up in a self-imposed jail five days a week. That's why I wrote this book. You see, I'm an Escape Artist. I help people – people just like you – escape from Professional Prison and find Professional Paradise. I believe *work* is NOT a four-letter word! I believe you can be a superstar *and* find fulfillment *and* be happy at work.

Now you may be wondering, "What's in it for me to seek Professional Paradise?" Do you mean other than **less stress, more energy and remarkable results**? You need more? Well, it's a good thing there are a number of benefits to an extended stay in Professional Paradise:

+ Increased productivity;

+ Improved creativity;

+ More effective problem solving;

+ Better working relationships and communication;

+ Enhanced health (lower blood pressure, more restful sleep, reduced incidence of common illnesses and serious diseases);

+ More financial rewards (bonuses, commissions, raises);

+ Additional smiles and laughter.

In this book, not only will I give you the keys that will free you from Professional Prison, but I will also hand you your Passport to Professional Paradise. I'll show you step by step how you can live the good life at work using a proven, proprietary technique called **SHIFT** that's already being used by many people to find their bliss. The five steps of the *SHIFT* technique are simple but not necessarily easy, common sense but not common practice.

Let's face it. There are a lot of things you have no control over that affect your job satisfaction – things like your responsibilities and duties, your salary, your hours, your boss, etc. These elements are, for the most part, pre-determined. But I'm here to tell you that those things don't determine the quality of your work experience. **Professional Paradise has little to do with your career, your coworkers, your company, the commute or the cash. You – and you alone – determine whether you will reside in Professional Prison, Professional Paradise or someplace in between.**

"Darn it!" I can hear you now! You were thinking you could blame your prison sentence on *someone* or *something* else (such as the boss, customers, coworkers or the company).

No such luck! It all comes down to you. Don't you hate that? Well, you should love it! Why? Because it means *you* are in control. You have the choice and the ability to create a Professional Paradise you've never even imagined until now, no matter what you do or where you work. And you can do it right now, today.

If you doubt the concept of Professional Paradise, that's fine. For now, I'm asking you to simply be open to the possibility that Professional Paradise exists. Surely you have at least one friend who loves his or her job and would describe it as Professional Paradise. Keep this person in mind as you read. Think of how happy he or she sounds when you ask, "How's work?"

Finding Professional Paradise is not only possible, it's a certainty – *if* you're willing to make a few changes. You may be skeptical that any of this is possible and that's okay. You don't have to believe yet. You just have to do one thing: **Pack your bags!**

PART I

PARADISE...PRISON...
OR SOMEWHERE IN BETWEEN?

Palm Trees and a Warm Breeze

~~~~~~~~~~~~~~~~~~~~~~~~~~~~

Where is *your* Professional Paradise?

We were on the airplane making our final approach into the island airport. My husband, Alan, and I looked at each other and smiled.

We'd spent months planning this trip…scheduling time off from work, finding someone to care for the children, coordinating household logistical issues, and of course, setting up all the travel arrangements. At last we were on vacation – peering out the window at the postcard perfect view below: crystal clear skies, sapphire-blue water, emerald-green vegetation, miles of pristine beaches and the majesty of the mountains rising up from the interior of the island.

"Wow," I thought. "Now this is paradise!"

Paradise. The word has existed in some form or fashion since the 12th century and has evolved through the Iranian, Greek, Latin and French languages. The earliest meaning referred to extraordinary walled gardens or royal hunting grounds. But check any modern English dictionary, and you'll find the contemporary definition of

13

paradise: *a place known for favorable conditions, special opportunities and abundance; a state of supreme happiness, delight or bliss.*

What could be better than that?

When I hear the word "paradise," of course I remember my tropical heaven on earth. And I think many people have that same notion of paradise – an exotic locale where the sun always shines and life comes easily. But others have a completely different idea of paradise. For them, it might be the thrill of rafting down a wild river canyon, spending the day being pampered at a luxurious spa, shooting under par at Pebble Beach or conquering a double-black-diamond slope with fresh powder. Or perhaps the good life is curling up with a great book in front of a roaring fire, driving a precision sports car on the open road, savoring a five-course gourmet meal or catching lightning bugs with the kids at dusk on a summer evening.

What does paradise mean to you?

Sit back, close your eyes (after you read this paragraph, of course) and visualize your version of paradise. Take a few deep breaths and let the feeling of paradise wash over you. Relax and enjoy as you use all of your senses to experience your nirvana....

At this point, you're likely thinking, "Forget about work! I'm going to paradise!"

Before you run out the door, let me ask you a question: **Why can't you have paradise** *at work?* Why can't you live the good life right where you are?

If you're like most people, you want to believe it's possible but you're skeptical. After all, work isn't supposed to be pleasant. They call it work for a reason, right? You wonder, "Is there really such a thing as *Professional* Paradise? Does it exist?"

Absolutely! Your job can, in fact, involve "favorable conditions, special opportunities and abundance." You can experience "a state of supreme happiness, delight or bliss" every day at work.

When you're in Professional Paradise you genuinely enjoy each day. You are at ease – focused and energized. You work to your strengths, routinely perform at your peak and effortlessly produce results. Your interactions with coworkers and customers are positive and productive. If you have to work for a living, what could be better than that?

Perhaps you're thinking that Professional Paradise comes from working for a particular company or having a certain job. This is most definitely *not* true. **Professional Paradise is a state of being – a state of mind backed up with intentional action.** So often it's not what happens at work, but how we perceive it, think about it and act on it that has a lasting impact.

Consider this: Have you – or someone you know – ever had a fantastic job with a great company making incredible money and yet you didn't feel like you were in Professional Paradise? It happens all the time. Maybe you weren't reaching your potential or you didn't enjoy the people you worked with or you weren't given the resources you needed to perform your job effectively.

Professional Paradise is not tied to a specific job, company, position or process. Rather, it is tied directly to your state of mind. When I was in my twenties and worked as a sales trainer for a computer company, I loved traveling for my job. I was on the road two to three times each month for two or three days at a time. I had the opportunity to visit new cities, see the sights and visit out-of-town friends. And, of course, I got my work done. This was Professional Paradise for me.

Fast forward ten years and add a husband, two children and a dog. That same training job with all the traveling would have been the opposite of Professional Paradise – what I call Professional Prison. The job, the work, the company…none of it changed. What changed was my perspective or mindset.

Am I starting to convince you yet?

Rest assured, Professional Paradise is not a mirage or some version of Fantasy Island. In fact, it's grounded in scientific study. Teresa Amabile and Steven Kramer report in *Harvard Business Review* that performance is driven by our state of mind. Their research, based on more than 12,000 diary entries by workers over three years, shows a direct connection between employees' inner lives – including their perceptions and emotions – and performance: "People perform better when their workday experiences include more positive emotions, stronger intrinsic motivation (passion for work), and more favorable perceptions of their work, their team, their leaders, and their organization." In other words, we all do better at work when we have a positive perspective. This seems like common sense, but it's nice to know that scientific research has actually proven the point.

Furthermore, in a *Time* magazine cover story "The Science of Happiness," Richard Davidson (known as "the king of happiness research") says, "Happiness isn't just a vague, ineffable feeling; it's a physical state of the brain – *one that you can induce deliberately*." Since paradise is defined as supreme happiness, this research is good news! It means **you don't have to depend on others for your happiness or your paradise. You can create it yourself** – on a regular basis – even at work!

You'll soon discover that I'm an insatiably curious person. I love to ask questions, conduct informal surveys and do research with my clients. I've asked more than one thousand people what makes them happy at work – what experiences create delight and bliss. The responses vary from getting the job done effectively to laughing with coworkers. I vividly remember one woman who simply answered, "I would like to be able to say 'I like my job' and mean it."

So what makes people happy at work?

30%	Successfully completing a task or project
15%	Positive connections with coworkers and customers
15%	Receiving appreciation from others
12%	Teamwork
12%	Money
16%	Various other responses

Notice that no one listed "doing as little as possible" or "surfing the web" or "shooting the breeze by the water cooler" as their nirvana. Notice, too, that "money" was mentioned by only a small percentage of people. What do you think about the data?

I'm psyched! I love that people think that getting their work done is important. These results (as well as the research cited earlier) support what I have long believed to be true – that Professional Paradise is determined not by external factors but by *internal* factors. The meaning and value of *success, positive connections, appreciation, teamwork* and even *money* are in the eye of the beholder. Do you see how this list is closely connected to your state of mind and not actual events?

Ultimately, your perspective determines your satisfaction. According to a recent report by global consulting giant Blessing White, employee engagement – which I think of as Professional Paradise – is individualized. Why? Because **work is personal**. Our perspectives, as well as our likes and dislikes, are unique. Let's look at some real-life examples.

Sheila is a physical therapist who values professional development and growth. For her, Professional Paradise is learning about new treatment options and then using them with her clients to provide better patient outcomes. She actually enjoys the extra time spent digging deep into medical journals and the internet to find best practices.

Steve, an IT professional, believes he's living the good life when his customers put their trust in him to fix major system glitches. He sees complex technical problems as interesting puzzles to be solved. While other people might resent being in the field without much support, Steve loves the autonomy and independence.

How about you? Would you find paradise in Sheila's or Steve's situation? What does living the good life at work mean to you? If you let yourself dream about an ideal day in Professional Paradise, what picture would you paint? What story would you tell?

Here's my description of Professional Paradise:

I see: *People laughing, people who "get it"*

I hear: *Interesting dialogue and discussion about the topic at hand*

I think: *"I'm so blessed to get to do this every day."*

I say: *"How can I be of service?"*

> I feel: *Hope, joy, contentment, enthusiasm, positive emotions*
>
> I experience: *Learning, creating new ideas, connecting people together, serving others*
>
> I connect with: *Like-minded people who sparkle and shine with enthusiasm, people who need a "shot in the arm" to get themselves back on track*

My Professional Paradise: *Helping other people escape from Professional Prison and find their way to their own Professional Paradise*

Take a moment now to really think about your Professional Paradise. The first step to achieving anything you desire in life is to paint a clear picture of the end result. It's well worth your time, energy and effort to get perfectly clear about what you are striving for. Once again, sit back, close your eyes, take a few deep breaths and use all of your senses to visualize a day in Professional Paradise. Remember, workplace Utopia is different for everyone. There's no right or wrong answer. Go with what feels "true" to you.

Do you have it? Great! Now write down your thoughts below. (The act of writing gives value to the ideas and creates momentum.)

I see: _____

I hear: _____

I think: _____

I say: _____

I feel: _____

I experience: _____

I connect with: _____

My Professional
Paradise: _____

Perhaps you're thinking, "This sounds great, Vicki. But is it realistic? Can I really get to Professional Paradise?"

Almost everyone can find Shangri-La at work through a *SHIFT* in viewpoint, thoughts and actions. (There are a few souls who are truly trapped in horrendous work environments where no amount of *SHIFT*ing will help. For them, the path to paradise starts with the words "I quit.")

I'll say it again because it bears repeating – the Professional Paradise you seek is not dependent on your job, your boss, your customers or your coworkers. It is dependent on your inner world (your mindset, thoughts and viewpoint) more than your outer world. That might lead some people to think that getting to Professional Paradise is about positive thinking. That's a good start, but it's much more than that. You won't achieve less stress, more energy and remarkable results simply by changing the way you think. You have to take action to put your thoughts into practice. Your mindset drives your actions which in turn drive outcomes.

MINDSET ⟶ ACTIONS ⟶ OUTCOMES

You can find Professional Paradise in most any work situation, *if* you're willing to open your mind and take some action. Are you ready?

Jailhouse Blues

Doin' time in Professional Prison

Picture a prison. What comes to mind?

Barbed wire…bars…locks…cold, bare cells…orange jumpsuits…guns…
threatening people…surly guards…confinement…hopelessness…despair.

It's not a pretty picture.

It's hard to imagine that these images could be related to work,
but unfortunately, too many people feel like they're doing time in
Professional Prison. In fact, a recently released report on employee
loyalty from Walker Information (published in Harvard Business
Online) states that approximately 25 percent of employees "feel
trapped in their jobs."

Like Professional Paradise, Professional Prison is not a physical place.
Instead, it's a state of being – **a certain mindset that drives
unproductive actions and, ultimately, undesirable outcomes**.
And, just like Professional Paradise, it's a function of internal drivers
more than external drivers. Those who perceive that they're trapped

at work create their own mental barbed wire and lockdowns that keep them imprisoned. They often see others as threatening or ominous (like inmates) instead of helpful and supportive. They view a complaining customer, challenging coworker or difficult boss as someone who is out to get them personally, much like the bully in the prison exercise yard. As a result, they're always waiting for the other shoe to drop, so to speak. In their world, anxiety and uncertainty are the common elements of each day.

Sometimes, people in Professional Prison put themselves in solitary confinement. They keep to themselves and want others to leave them alone so they can "do their jobs in peace." These individuals believe that avoiding other people will make their life easier. I'll never forget the time I was training customer service reps in a call center, and one of the participants said (*and she meant it*), "This job would be great if it weren't for the customers." Sounds like she'd sentenced herself to 20-years-to-life!

Then there are those who join the "chain gang" at work. People stuck in Professional Prison want company. After all, it can get lonely in lockup! These Professional Prisoners are drawn to each other because they enjoy commiserating with people who are just as unhappy as they are. Sometimes, they even try to "recruit" more contented coworkers. When Prisoners get around peers who are teetering between Paradise and Prison, they tend to crank up the rumor mill, spread malicious gossip, put a negative spin on good news and criticize everything the organization or senior leadership does. This is often done without conscious thought, but that doesn't make it any less dangerous. Do you have a chain gang in your workplace?

To be sure, there are different "degrees" of Professional Prison. Some people feel as if they've been sentenced to life in a maximum security facility. Maybe they work in an especially high-stress profession or their job requires that they work long, arduous hours. Or perhaps they have a boss who is perpetually unfair and unreasonable. These are external factors that can be difficult to improve without changing careers, jobs or organizations. However, know this: **It is possible to adjust your perspective about external factors to make them more tolerable if you choose to do so.** The strategies you'll discover throughout this book will help you do just that.

Another degree of Professional Prison is similar to "sleeping one off" in the county jail. Although this still involves being "behind bars" (metaphorically speaking, of course), the sentence is short, and before long the Professional Prisoner is free. An example of this is having a massive project with a looming deadline. It's one of those times when you think, "There's no way I can get this done – there just aren't enough hours in the day." You feel trapped, panic-stricken, but you have no choice except to suffer through and work day and night until it's done.

If you've ever done a stint in Professional Prison (and who hasn't?), you likely felt stuck in your job. You probably experienced relentless pressure, a lack of energy, maybe even sheer misery. Perhaps you were endlessly negative, complained about everything, overreacted to situations or became easily overwhelmed. You might have found yourself calling in sick when you weren't ill or dreaming of greener grass in some other company.

Do you regularly suffer from the Sunday Night Blues – that awful feeling you get in the pit of your stomach about 5:00 on Sunday afternoon when you realize you have to go back to work tomorrow? You think, "Only five days until Friday." This is a sure sign of being locked in Professional Prison.

If you stay in Professional Prison long enough, you soon forget what freedom feels like. Over time, you become hopeless, resigned to your plight as a Prisoner, and you start to think that these feelings are normal. Eventually you accept the four walls of your "cell" as a dead end, and you settle into a self-imposed life sentence. Think about literally being stuck or locked up. After a while, you'd physically experience the effects of being trapped – you'd likely feel anxious, panicky and out of control. That's why many people who stay in Professional Prison long term suffer from chronic stress-related illnesses like headaches, panic attacks, ulcers, high blood pressure and back problems.

Here's what's really interesting: Many people, when challenged to do something about their prisoner status, say things like, "I don't have a choice" or "What am I supposed to do about it?" They see themselves as victims and believe that their prison sentence was imposed by someone or something else. But remember, Professional Prison is not about where you work or what you do; it's a reflection of how you view your work. To prove my point, following is an example of two different people in the same work situation. One is in Professional Prison while the other is living the good life at work.

Sam is a salesperson in a regional office products company. Sam's new boss, Marco, is younger than he is and has only been with the company a few months. Marco has an impressive resume and was the top choice for the manager position. Sam even participated in the interviewing process and recommended Marco.

However, just a few weeks after Marco started, Sam began to feel micromanaged. Marco's attention to detail and constant follow-up were suffocating. Sam was used to operating independently – he and his former boss had an informal agreement that Sam would be left alone as long as he produced results. He'd really liked his job until all this "under the microscope" business began. Each time Marco asked Sam a question about an account, Sam grew more resentful and angry. He saw these questions as a direct assault on his character, work ethic and proven performance. Soon, even small questions that Sam wouldn't have noticed in the past became incredibly annoying. Just three months into Marco's leadership, Sam felt "sentenced" to his job. He was locked in Professional Prison.

One of Sam's coworkers, Ravi, was also involved in the interviewing process and thought Marco was a good choice. Ravi was particularly happy that a new manager was coming on board because he felt like his last boss was never around and didn't support the salespeople. You can probably guess what happened next: Ravi welcomed Marco's management style. Ravi saw it as coaching and mentoring rather than micro-managing. Each time Marco checked in, Ravi took advantage of the opportunity to forge a strong relationship, seek his advice and learn new elements of the job. Ravi appreciated the assistance and was motivated by his boss's attention. He saw opportunity where Sam saw only frustration. For Ravi, this was Professional Paradise.

Neither salesman was right or wrong. Sam's and Ravi's perspectives of Marco's leadership style were vastly different. As a result, they had completely opposite mindsets about work. This is a perfect example of how your mindset is such a strong influence on your ability to live the good life at work.

Just as different people have different ideas about Professional Paradise, so it is with Professional Prison. Everyone sees it differently. What would Professional Prison look like to you? Stop right now and take a few minutes to experience it using the same techniques you used to visualize your Professional Paradise. It's crucial to identify Professional Prison so you can recognize it should you start to spend too much time there.

Now jot down your thoughts:

I see: _____

I hear: _____

I think: _____

I say: _____

I feel: _____

I experience: _____

I don't connect with: _____

My Professional Prison: _____

Clearly, Prison is not where you want to be! It makes you wonder, "Why do people stay locked up in Professional Prison when they could be enjoying Paradise instead?"

To be sure, some organizations and leaders make it tough to get to Paradise. They may even perpetuate a Prison mentality through a variety of less-than-thoughtful employment practices such as unfair pay structures, unrealistic expectations regarding workload and hours, or lack of respect for employees. You may be powerless to change these things, but you can change your response to them. That's the *only* way to change the outcomes and results you experience every day on the job.

I've found that people often continue to work in Professional Prison because it's the path of least resistance…it's comfortable. I know this sounds crazy – how can "prison" and "comfortable" appear in the same sentence? It's called *institutionalization*: the process by which real inmates becomes so accustomed to the four walls, three meals and structure of prison life that they actually prefer it over freedom.

For the Professional Prisoner, sometimes it's simply easier to maintain a self-imposed prison sentence than do what it takes to escape. Mentally staying put and being miserable is the path of least resistance. This may sound counterintuitive, but look around, and you'll notice it happening all over the place. Think about the Dilbert® cartoon – a whole consumer-driven product line has been created to complain about work.

I'll bet some of you are thinking, "That's not me. Why would I want to stay trapped in Prison?" or "You don't understand – I have my reasons why I can't make any changes at work."

You have every right to stay locked up if that's what you want. You also have the opportunity to get on the path to less stress, more energy and remarkable results at work. Remember, both Prison and Paradise are states of being. You have a choice about your mindset and your actions.

Whether you've been wrongly convicted, you're in a prison of your own making or you're a repeat offender, you can continue in Professional Prison or you can make a daring escape and head to Professional Paradise. Where would you rather be?

Put your objections on the back burner and keep reading with an open mind. You might just discover that you've had the key to your freedom all along.

Out on Parole

~~~~~~

Are you a Professional Parolee?

So far, you've created your vision of Professional Paradise and identified your nightmare of Professional Prison. Now the question is, where do you spend most of your time – in Professional Prison, Professional Paradise or somewhere in between?

Carefully think about your typical daily work experience – not your best day or your worst day. Try to be objective and avoid any judgment as you formulate your answer – it's important that you answer honestly. Then draw a vertical line on the Prison-Paradise Continuum below that best illustrates where you are:

**Professional
Prison**

**Professional
Paradise**

Are you already living the good life at work – having fun and basking in the sun in Paradise? If so, congratulations! But don't stop here… keep reading. Why? Because the strategies you'll learn in Part II will make it easier for you to stay in Paradise and make your time there even more rewarding.

If this exercise has confirmed what you've been feeling in your gut — that you're stuck in Prison — don't despair. Just keep reading. *Please, please* keep reading. I truly believe the *SHIFT* steps will give you the perspective change and the tools you need to escape. Too often, people think they have to quit their jobs in order to get out of Prison. Before you go changing jobs, try changing your *mindset* about your job. Sometimes that makes all the difference.

But what if you're neither in Prison nor in Paradise? If you placed yourself somewhere in the middle, you're on what I call Professional Parole. *Merriam-Webster's Dictionary of Law* defines parole as "the state of freedom resulting from a conditional release of a prisoner who has served part of a sentence and who remains under the control of and in the legal custody of a parole authority." Being out on parole is a whole lot better than being in prison, but a parolee is not completely free…he can't leave town, and he certainly can't jet off to paradise.

Professional Parole is a similar concept. You're not so miserable that you feel completely trapped in Professional Prison, thank goodness, but you're not "free" and living the good life at work either. Some days you're productive and in the zone; others days are spent moving slowly and watching the clock. There are many great things about your job as well as some big frustrations. Professional Parole is — you guessed it — a state of being, **an apathetic mindset that leads to reaction instead of proactive action.** Things aren't bad enough to make you quit, but they're unpleasant enough for you to feel the suffering in some form or fashion.

You know you're on Parole when you've lost the skip in your step. Maybe you have chronic mild stress and find yourself complaining about little things that never bothered you before like occasionally having to stay late, a messy common area, vacillating thermostats or a minor change in parking arrangements. Staff meetings and company gatherings aren't as motivating or fun as they used to be, and you go because you have to, not because you want to. You likely spend a lot of time questioning your value to the team or organization, and you may have that nagging feeling that you're wasting your potential, that there *must* be something more to life.

Does any of this feel familiar?

If so, you're not alone. Most people are on Professional Parole. My research indicates that a small percentage of people truly feel trapped in their jobs every day, a slightly larger percentage truly live the good life at work, and the vast majority are stuck in Limbo Land. And it seems my findings are supported by other studies. Based on a survey by the Gallup Organization, over half of today's workers are on Professional Parole. Gallup's results indicate that 16 percent of the U.S. workforce is actively disengaged (Professional Prison), 29 percent is engaged (Professional Paradise) and 55 percent is not engaged (Professional Parole).

Why so many people on Parole? Some have managed to escape from Prison. For them, Parole is simply the next step. Others began their careers or jobs in Paradise, but over time it slipped away from them. They've tasted the good life at work, and they believe they can have it again...they're just not sure how to get it back. Then there are those who've been on Parole their entire careers. Their work experiences have always been just so-so because their negative beliefs about work drive their perceptions and, therefore, their outcomes.

Let's look at some real-life Parolees. Janel is director of research for a global financial services firm. She has flexible work hours and a fantastic compensation package, works from her home in a small beach town and has good support from the corporate office. Sounds like Professional Paradise, doesn't it? Well, in recent months, Janel has been discontent and disengaged. She told me, "I need more connection with people – I practically work in seclusion. And I need some kind of professional development or growth." She doesn't want to change jobs as much as she wants to fix a few aspects of her job that bother her.

Marlene is a pharmaceutical sales rep. She works part time and makes good money. Six months ago her territory was enlarged, substantially increasing her drive time. She went from calling on doctors' offices in her hometown of Wilmington, DE, to making almost daily trips to Philadelphia, sitting for hours in traffic. She genuinely likes what she does and the people she works with, but she dreads the increased driving. Now she plods through the day, complaining and feeling sorry for herself. She's on Professional Parole.

And then there's Carlos, a logistics expert. When I asked him how he feels about his job, he said, "Let me put it this way: Most of my coworkers go to lunch around 11:30. I purposely wait and go later in the day so the afternoons go by faster. I figure if I can just make it to lunch, the rest of the day won't be so bad." Yikes!

How would you describe Professional Parole? Jot down a few words or phrases here.

Professional Parole feels like...

_____

_____

_____

The next logical question is, why do people *stay* on Parole? In some cases, for the same reason people stay in Prison: It's the path of least resistance. But when it comes to Parole, I think there are four other reasons why most of us stay put.

The first is **fear**. Fear is a great immobilizer. Too many people won't even let themselves imagine Professional Paradise because they don't want to be disappointed. Their internal voices knock them down with fear and uncertainty. "What if I take this promotion, and I don't like being a manager?" "What if I look at things differently and it backfires?" Not too long ago, I met an accounts payable clerk who was highly dedicated and possessed great job skills. She'd been in the same position for a number of years, and work felt stale and mundane. I suggested she apply for an open job in her department that involved additional responsibilities. Her response? "I'm afraid. What if I can't do the new job?"

Some people are Parolees for life because they have **low expectations**. They hold deeply entrenched beliefs that work is something you endure. They've watched their parents, loved ones or role models go to work day after day for nothing more than the paycheck. And because they think being unhappy at work is standard operating procedure, they don't even know they have a choice. If you don't know Paradise exists, Parole doesn't look so bad compared to Prison.

The third reason is a **lack of personal accountability**. Ouch! That one hurt! But if we want to get to Paradise, we have to be brutally honest with ourselves. Let's face it, most of us don't want to accept the fact that the quality of our work experience truly is up to us. It's a whole lot easier to blame our boss, our coworkers, our company or some other factor than to accept responsibility for where we are. It takes courage and strength to admit that it's our fault we've been unhappy or just biding time in a job for months or even years. That's a bitter pill to swallow for anyone. When was the last time you checked in with yourself about your priorities and career goals? Have you lost touch with the "old you" who was energized and engaged at work?

Although your manager and your organization obviously have an impact on your work experience, they are not the reason you're disengaged, nor are they responsible for engaging you. *You* are responsible for engaging you. **You are the Chief Paradise Officer (CPO) of your own life**. It's up to you to create your own Professional Paradise. You have a choice: do nothing and stay on Parole, slide backwards into Prison, or *SHIFT* towards Paradise.

And that brings us to the final reason why so many people never get off Parole – **they simply don't know how**. I believe that many people genuinely want less stress, more energy and remarkable results at work and are ready to take control, but they don't have the tools to make it happen. Fortunately, this book has the solution. The first step is to get off Parole using the *SHIFT* steps I'll share with you. Then you can go one better and head toward your own Shangri-La at work.

POWs and WOWs

The signs of Prison and Paradise

Like many situations in life, where you are in your work experience is not the result of a few major events, but rather the accumulation of many minor events over time. Take, for instance, the institution of marriage. A loving, enduring relationship is built over a period of years through many daily choices that reflect how much the spouses respect, support and treat each other. Likewise, a few big fights don't push a couple to divorce. Behind every failed marriage is a mountain of seemingly insignificant arguments, countless misunderstandings, scores of disappointments and years of distrust.

People who find themselves in actual prison and paradise don't suddenly appear there. Although a single illegal act may be the culminating event that finally lands a criminal in prison, it's usually the result of a myriad of bad influences and years of delinquency. Independently wealthy people who live the good life every day likely didn't win the lottery and find themselves in paradise the next day. Most got there through years of hard work, innumerable brilliant business decisions and prudent financial choices.

And so it is at work.

It is the compounding of many individual events, situations, interactions and experiences that puts us in Prison, Paradise or somewhere in between. I call these factors POWs and WOWs, depending on whether they are essentially negative or positive. Let's take a closer look at each one.

The Random House Unabridged Dictionary tells us that a pow is "a heavy blow." Have you ever experienced a figurative heavy blow at work — an event, situation or interaction that sucker punches you, distracts you, aggravates you and just plain leaves you feeling bad? That's a POW in a nutshell. It's something bad or negative that happens to you — a metaphorical body blow or right uppercut to the chin.

Think of a POW you've recently experienced. How did it make you feel?

POWs are either *internally* or *externally* generated. Internal POWs are self-inflicted, created by you, such as showing up late for a meeting to find everyone waiting on you, losing a sale because you weren't prepared or making a careless mistake on a report. Some internal POWs come from your mindset — how you perceive things and react to them. Being so worried about a situation that you can't focus on your work or assuming a colleague is blowing you off because he or she hasn't responded to your email are good examples.

External POWs, on the other hand, are the result of non-controllable situations or other people's actions. They happen *to* you instead of *within* you. Examples might include a traffic jam that makes you late for an appointment, a copier that breaks down minutes before the report is due, or a PDA that quits working on a business trip. Many of the external POWs we experience are related to change, lack of control or rules and regulations.

POWs caused by other people can originate with customers, vendors, competitors, coworkers, direct reports or leaders. For instance, an angry customer calls to complain, one of your team members is out sick during crunch time, or the supplier suddenly announces they can't meet your deadline. Leaders and staff alike experience POWs. Think of the department head who learns from the vice president that her financial goals for the quarter have been raised without her input or the company that discovers its competitor has launched an innovative new product. See the chart on the next page for more examples of POWs.

Internal POWs
Procrastination; poor time management
Fear; lack of confidence
Not meeting goals, objectives, deadlines
Lack of knowledge or skills
Indecisiveness
Lack of commitment or focus
Being disorganized
Making mistakes; lack of attention to detail

External POWs	
With Coworkers	**With Customers**
Poor or no communication	Complaints
Uncertainties of a new boss or team member	Not returning calls or calling too often
Poor performance by others that negatively impacts you	Lost sales
Differing opinions; conflicting priorities, goals or sense of urgency	Unrealistic/unreasonable expectations
Lack of recognition from leaders or peers	Changing scope or specifications
Interruptions	Project delays
Gossip	Quality concerns
Direct reports who don't share important news	Pricing issues

When you get hit with a POW, either you get riled up or you shut down. It's the innate "fight or flight" reaction. You might get angry or annoyed, or become filled with anxiety. POWs sap your energy and enthusiasm, and leave you feeling disheartened, disappointed, distrustful and disengaged. You often experience physical changes as well. Your heart rate increases, your blood pressure might shoot up and your palms start to sweat.

When POWs pile up day after day, you become imprisoned. Over time, the negative events, thoughts and reactions lead to a sense of hopelessness and create the feeling of being trapped. A few POWs here and there are no big deal. Everyone – even those in Paradise – experience POWs from time to time. It's the perpetual presence of POWs that packs you into Professional Prison.

POWs are like ripples in a pond – their impact extends beyond you to affect coworkers, customers, teams, even entire organizations. Think of a recent encounter where a teammate perhaps overreacted, jumped all over you and then apologized, saying something like, "Sorry. I'm in a bad mood because (fill in the blank)." That's the ripple effect of POWs.

What POWs do you frequently experience at work? In the space on the following page, write down three common POWs you get hit with and identify each one as internal or external.

POW	Internal?	External?
Example: Forgetting materials for a client meeting	✓	
Example: Your coworker forgets materials for a client meeting		✓

Notice that the outcome is the same in the two example POWs, even though one is internal and one is external – there are no materials for that important meeting! If *you* forget the materials, you might beat yourself up over your mistake. The situation plays out differently if it's your coworker who forgets the materials. You'd likely still be angry, but you'd blame your coworker. Either way, you have a client meeting to save. And either way, you can control your reaction and find a solution using the *SHIFT* steps.

Look back at your external POWs. Are they within your control? Probably not. But guess what? *It doesn't matter!* What is within your control is how you respond to them – your mindset and your actions. That may sound idealistic, but it doesn't mean it isn't true.

Now let's *SHIFT* gears (pun intended) to something a little more pleasant…

You just got the call. The deal you've been trying to close finally came through! *WOW!*

At last, the project your team has been focusing on for weeks is complete – on time and under budget! *WOW!*

Interesting…you've just learned a new computer program that will save you hours of time! *WOW!*

A *wow* is a joyous exclamation. *Merriam-Webster Dictionary* also defines it as "a sensational hit or a striking success." A WOW as I define it is any sensationally successful event, situation, interaction or experience that creates a positive outcome, result or emotion. WOWs get you jazzed. They create joy, delight and pleasure. When you have a WOW, you feel like you're in the zone, at the top of your game, performing at your peak. You are energized, your stress level is low, and you have a skip in your step.

Think of a WOW you've recently experienced. How did it make you feel?

Have you ever noticed that when you say "WOW!" you automatically smile? Say it aloud right now and see what happens. You just have to smile because of how your mouth forms the letters. Pretty cool, isn't it?

Like POWs, WOWs can be either internal or external. Internal WOWs come from your viewpoint or your response to certain things, such as noticing a stunning sunset while you're sitting in traffic or feeling fulfilled when you serve someone else (even if they don't notice). One of my favorite internal WOWs is solving a problem or coming up with a great idea all on my own. Now that feels good!

External WOWs come from other people or situations. A WOW could be a surprise bonus or raise, a coworker pitching in to help you on a busy day, or a senior executive publicly acknowledging your efforts at a staff meeting.

Internal WOWs
☺ Finishing tasks and projects
☺ Learning a new skill
☺ Hitting goals and achieving results
☺ Finding creative solutions
☺ Laughter and fun
☺ Getting paid what you think you're worth
☺ Problem solving
☺ Using your talents and strengths

External WOWs	
With Coworkers	**With Customers**
☺ Teamwork and synergy	☺ Closing sales
☺ Helping or mentoring one another	☺ Returned calls
☺ Appreciation from teammates or your boss	☺ Happy, easy-going clients
☺ Personal accountability or initiative by direct reports and coworkers	☺ Solving client problems and issues
☺ Creative problem solving	☺ Referrals and repeat business
☺ Being given an exciting new responsibility or opportunity	☺ Fair negotiations
☺ Freedom and autonomy	☺ Appreciation from customers
☺ Positive interactions with others	☺ Positive reactions to ideas

Which WOWs click with you? Take a moment now to jot down three common WOWs that get you jazzed and then indicate whether each is internally or externally driven.

WOW	Internal?	External?
Example: You just finished a project, and you give yourself a big pat on the back!	✓	
Example: You just finished a project, and your boss gives you a big pat on the back!		✓

Did you have more internal or external WOWs? Interestingly, people tend to *notice* internal WOWs more than external ones because we're often not "present" enough in the moment to recognize the external ones. I have a friend who is always so busy thinking about the next project or assignment that she genuinely doesn't hear the accolades she receives from her boss and teammates. As a result, she feels unappreciated when in fact the opposite is true. What WOWs have you missed lately?

As you've probably guessed, an accumulation of WOWs puts you squarely in Professional Paradise. When you consistently experience

WOWs on a daily basis, you'll find that you are absolutely living the good life at work.

You've probably also surmised that you're on Professional Parole when you regularly experience both POWs and WOWs. Remember our description of Parole – some good stuff, some bad stuff; some good days, some bad days. That back and forth is the result of POWs and WOWs.

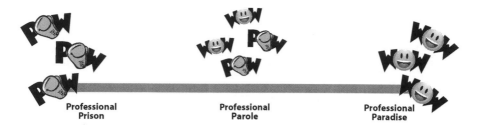

Professional Prison   Professional Parole   Professional Paradise

Where you are on the Prison–Parole–Paradise continuum is subjective and personal. One POW doesn't land you in Prison; one WOW doesn't put you in Paradise. Just like the marriage example at the beginning of this chapter, **it's the cumulative effect of many individual POWs and WOWs that determines the quality of your work experience**.

Right now you might be asking the million dollar question: "How many WOWs does it take to get to Professional Paradise?" Great news! That is up to you to decide. Just as you created your own vision of Professional Paradise in Chapter 1, *you* determine when you've arrived there. Generally speaking though, it's relative. When you steadily experience significantly more WOWs than POWs you'll be on your way.

Here's an analogy that might help you put POWs and WOWs in perspective: Imagine that you're standing in the middle of a vast field of dead weeds. It's an ugly sight. You bend down and pull a weed. In its place, you plant a flower seed. You continue to work your way through the field, pulling weeds and planting seeds. Now this is one huge field, so you come back day after day, pulling weeds and planting seeds. Before long, you start to notice a difference. The flowers are starting to grow and bloom. At first, there are just a few scattered among the weeds. But as time goes on, the flowers start to overtake the weeds. You keep pulling and planting, pulling and planting. The more flowers you see, the more you pull and plant. Then, one day, you return to the field to a truly magnificent site... flowers as far as the eye can see. Yes, there are still a few weeds here and there, but you don't notice them. The beauty and fragrance of thousands of flowers is enchanting and consuming.

That's how I see the transition from Professional Prison to Professional Paradise. Every time you *SHIFT* a POW to a WOW, it's like pulling a weed and replacing it with a flower seed. A WOW or two starts to pop up here and there. That's where it starts – one WOW at a time. You discover you like the WOWs, and you work to *SHIFT* even more POWs to WOWs. You're moving quickly towards Professional Parole. There are still some POWs, but you continue to replace them with WOWs. Until the day comes when the WOWs outnumber the POWs, and all you can see is the beauty of Professional Paradise. Get the picture?

POWs and WOWs are the individual pieces – the events, circumstances, situations and interactions – that, taken together, create Prison, Parole or Paradise. POWs and WOWs are the day-to-day evidence of where you are on your journey.

If you're in Prison or even on Parole, it may feel impossible to get to Paradise. But don't worry. In Part II, I'm going to teach you how to *SHIFT* your POWs to WOWs. Try *SHIFT*ing just one POW to a WOW with the simple, proven techniques I'm going to give you. Do you believe that you can transform one confrontation with a customer into a positive connection? Can you turn one personal mistake into a learning experience? Can you find one way to communicate better with your teammates? If you can do it once, then you can do it a hundred times — and then you're on your way to less stress, more energy and remarkable results at work.

PART II

SHIFT:
YOUR PASSPORT TO
PROFESSIONAL PARADISE

People who know me say I am Little Miss Glass-is-Overflowing. What can I tell you? I've been this way my whole life. I'm just a sunny person. I worked with a business consultant a few years back who helped me figure out just what makes me so optimistic. Is it simply in my DNA, or is it something I do?

After lots of great questions from the consultant and some extensive soul searching, I realized that, for me, living the good life both in my job and at home involves effort. Yes, some of it comes naturally, just like some people are naturally athletic. But even people without any natural talent can typically get good enough to play a sport and enjoy it.

Likewise, just about everyone can create their own Professional Paradise. It just takes determination and practice. Yet the effort is not unpleasant. You know how good you feel after a great workout at the gym? Well, you feel the same way when you work out your *SHIFT* muscles and transform your POWs to WOWs. The results are worth the effort.

And that brings us squarely to the "how-tos." So let's get started…

What is *SHIFT*?

SHIFT is an acronym that describes a series of steps you can use to transform any POW to a WOW. It's a proprietary technique I've developed over a number of years that simplifies the process of changing ineffective, detrimental thought patterns and actions into positive, beneficial thought patterns, actions and habits.

SHIFT is much more than just positive thinking. It's a way of looking at situations and events differently and making the necessary adjustments to create better outcomes. The steps are designed to help you discover where there are disconnects and make deliberate changes to get back on track. The benefits of using *SHIFT* are vastly improved productivity, performance and results, less stress, more energy and more positive connections with coworkers and customers. In short, the outcome is Professional Paradise!

The *SHIFT* methodology is proven. I've been sharing this concept for years, and thousands of people have learned and applied the principles. It works with and for everyone, regardless of age, gender or ethnicity. It works for every position and level in the organization — individual contributor, leader and senior executive. I've taught it in a wide array of industries, from healthcare to technology, commercial real estate to defense contractors. It works for any POW you might experience. It just plain works!

In this section, I'm going to teach you the five *SHIFT* steps in detail and then give you several opportunities to practice *SHIFT*ing with actual POWs you've experienced at work. However, the individual steps will make more sense if we first examine the *SHIFT* methodology on a macro level. To *SHIFT* POWs to WOWs and start living the good life at work, conceptually you must:

1. *SHIFT* your work beliefs.
2. *SHIFT* your mindset.
3. *SHIFT* your actions.
4. *SHIFT* your habits.

When you do these four things, your outcomes will *SHIFT* and your work experience will dramatically change for the better. The *SHIFT* process is truly transformational. It is, in fact, your Passport to Professional Paradise.

What You Believe is What You Receive

How your beliefs affect the quality of your work life

I've mentioned several times (repetition reinforces, right?) that Professional Paradise, Prison and Parole are products of your state of mind – outcomes of your internal world rather than your external world. When I first began developing the *SHIFT* technique, I was very curious about that. Why does one person see the sky as partly cloudy and another sees it as partly sunny? How can one team member think a coworker has a strong work ethic, while her teammate perceives the same coworker as lazy? Why do people see the exact same event, situation or interaction differently?

Now that's a complex question with a complex answer. Personality, individual preferences and mood are certainly key factors. But **the single most important factor in how we view the world is our belief system**. According to researcher Rogene Buchholz, "Beliefs define the world for an individual and constitute an information system to which a person looks for answers."

Beliefs are the foundation not only of our inner world, but also of our actions and reactions in the external world. Think back to the principle I shared in the first chapter about how your mindset drives your actions which drive your outcomes:

MINDSET ⟹ ACTIONS ⟹ OUTCOMES

Now we're going to expand that principle. When you experience some kind of event or situation (internal or external), that experience either creates a new belief, confirms an existing belief or contradicts an existing belief. The more your experiences confirm your beliefs, the more deeply entrenched they become. Conversely, the more your experiences contradict existing beliefs, the more likely you are to modify them. For example, if one of your direct reports misses a deadline on a critical analysis, it might confirm a belief that he or she – or employees in general – are not responsible. On the other hand, if all your direct reports consistently deliver on their commitments, you would likely start to change your belief about employees being irresponsible.

Your beliefs determine your state of mind (and your state of mind directs your actions which produce certain outcomes). Now here is where it gets interesting! The outcomes are, in effect, events or situations that either create new beliefs, or confirm or contradict existing beliefs. It's an ongoing cycle:

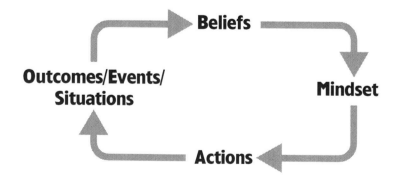

In the example on the previous page, the missed deadline (a POW) confirms your belief and makes you aggravated (your mindset). Your frustration drives you to set rigid due dates for all reports and to make your team work over the weekend (your action), which makes your direct reports resentful (the outcome). Despite the new guidelines – or perhaps because of them – your employees are now disgruntled and disengaged and still don't consistently meet deadlines, further reinforcing your belief that employees aren't responsible. The cycle continues…and so do the POWs!

Our *work* beliefs are the foundation of our mindset, actions and outcomes on the job. We all come to work with beliefs that act as a lens through which we see, experience and interpret every event, situation, interaction and circumstance. They are the "why" behind our thoughts and feelings at work.

Consider a work belief about punctuality and its importance (or lack thereof). Dee's work belief is "Good workers arrive on time," while Zack's work belief is "Good workers get the job done." In each case, the belief determines the mindset (be on time vs. okay to be late), which drives the actions (get to work on time vs. get to work whenever). If the rules or culture of this particular workplace dictate that either action is fine, then both Dee and Zack will likely have positive outcomes, such as being productive and feeling good about their work ethic. These WOWs contribute to a Paradise state of being and reinforce each person's notion that her/his work belief is correct. See how it plays out?

Differing work beliefs are the genesis of many challenges and conflicts in the workplace. Problems arise when our work beliefs are not in sync with the organization's values or when we work with others who don't share the same work beliefs. If Zack's tardiness affects Dee's performance (a big POW), then they need to create a positive solution that will work for both of them. If Dee is annoyed but her productivity isn't affected, then she should let it go. Either way, she can *SHIFT* the POW to a WOW and reduce her stress.

Many factors go into creating our belief system about work. Even the word work is full of extremes. Check any dictionary and the definition "employment or a vocation" is typically the first one you'll see. But keep looking and you'll find references to "toil," "effort" and "success." You know you're in trouble when the basic definition can lead to differing beliefs.

The primary inputs that establish our work beliefs are gender, cultural background, age or generation, upbringing, and personal work experiences. I could write an entire book on work beliefs, their origins and how they affect our ability to create Professional Paradise, but for the sake of brevity, let's take just a quick look at each of these factors. (If you'd like to learn more about this subject, visit www.ProfessionalParadise.com for a free *Belief Brief* white paper.)

Gender. We already know that gender is a compelling factor in communication style, relationships, our concept of success, our approach to problem solving, how we define our roles in life, and our notion of work/life balance…just to name a few! Is there anyone who *doesn't* think that gender is a compelling factor in the development of our work beliefs? I didn't think so. Enough said.

Cultural Background. As the world continues to shrink, we will undoubtedly find ourselves working more often with coworkers, suppliers and customers from other cultures and regions of the world. Traditions, values and business customs — which vary dramatically from culture to culture — have an enormous impact on work beliefs.

Age or Generation. Grandpa doesn't view the world the same way his iPod-carrying, text-messaging granddaughter does. The same is true in the workplace, where never before have so many people from different generations worked together at once. A workplace with Gen Y, Gen X and Baby Boomer employees is a perfect breeding ground for diverse work beliefs and therefore conflicting ideas about how and what should be done on any given day. The Baby Boomer's Professional Paradise could well be the Gen Y's Prison and vice versa.

Upbringing. Most people begin forming certain beliefs about work at a young age. As toddlers, we read books about firemen, nurses, teachers, business people and ballerinas. As we grew older, the messages we received about work continued throughout our school and college years. Our parents and teachers unwittingly planted ideas – some negative, some positive – about work and career throughout these formative years. An anonymous respondent to one of my mini-surveys about work beliefs learned from an early age that work stinks. The message in her house was "you work because you have to." On the other hand, a friend of mine learned growing up that work is enjoyable and something to look forward to. His father entertained him and his siblings with stories of the interesting people and exciting places he experienced while on the road as a traveling salesman in the food industry.

Personal Work Experiences. As we enter the workforce and begin to have our own positive and negative work experiences, our work beliefs evolve. In many cases, the beliefs we develop on our own are more powerful than the ones we learned growing up because the experiences they're based on directly impacted our emotions, our status, maybe even our wallets. Just the other day, I heard someone say, "You don't get to pick your job. You just need to get one and stick with it." *POW!* Obviously this person has some negative beliefs about choices and flexibility.

All of these different factors and influences – gender, cultural background, age, upbringing and personal experiences – come together to create a belief system that is the foundation of our work life.

Here's another response I received from my mini-survey: "My mother raised me as a single parent. We didn't have a lot of money, and she needed to work. I remember seeing her become physically ill before going to work. There was no love lost between her and her supervisor. She really dreaded going to work and dealing with him. As a child, seeing this really got to me. I didn't know much about work, other than it obviously wasn't pleasant. When I started working and then became a supervisor, I promised myself that I would create a work environment where everyone showed respect for one another." This is a profound example of how work beliefs affect not only our career choices and work experiences, but also the experiences of those we work with.

I hope you're starting to understand why your work beliefs are so important. Do you see how they can have a huge impact on your definition of Professional Paradise, Prison and Parole?

What are *your* work beliefs?

Identifying and recognizing your (often subconscious) work beliefs, assessing their value and consciously choosing to keep or *SHIFT* them is directly connected to your ability to get to Professional Paradise. Take a few minutes now to thoughtfully answer the following questions:

✦ How do you think your gender affects your beliefs about work?
What about your cultural heritage or ethnic background?

✦ Which generation do you belong to? How do you think that
impacts your work beliefs?

✦ Which two or three messages or beliefs about work did you
learn from parents, teachers or others when you were growing
up? For example: "Dad works; Mom stays at home" or "Never
trust the boss."

✦ What beliefs have you formed based on your own experiences
in the working world?

✦ How do all of these beliefs you've described impact you at work?

✦ Which harmful, detrimental beliefs do you need to *SHIFT* to more helpful, constructive beliefs?

Now that you've gained a better understanding of your own work beliefs, it's equally important to enhance your awareness of your coworkers' beliefs and to acknowledge that their beliefs are more than likely different from yours. Pay attention in conversations and meetings to others' actions and reactions, and consider how they might be based on an individualized set of beliefs. You can even ask your coworkers what beliefs they bring to work or start a discussion at a staff meeting. Teams function better and have more synergy when team members acknowledge and respect one another's unique point of view.

Let me now ask you the most important question of all: **Do you *truly believe* it's possible to create Professional Paradise and have less stress, more energy and remarkable results at work?**

The answer to that question is crucial. If you don't believe Professional Paradise is possible for you, the *SHIFT* steps will be far less effective because your belief system will work against them. You must truly believe that you can live the good life at work, or you'll never get to Professional Paradise. Why? Because **what you believe is what you receive!**

If you're already a believer, great! If not, that's okay too. There's nothing wrong with being skeptical. In fact, convinced skeptics often become the biggest believers. I challenge you to finish this book and then come back to this all important question.

From Alcatraz to Shangri-La

An overview of the *SHIFT* concept

We focused on identifying and *SHIFT*ing your work beliefs in the last chapter. Now let's give our attention to your mindset and your actions.

SHIFT Your Mindset

One of my favorite authors, Wayne Dyer, says in *The Power of Intention*, "When you change the way you look at things, the things you look at change." Please re-read that quote now and let its meaning soak in.

In essence, it means that when you change your perspective and your reaction to a situation, it has the *net effect* of changing the situation itself. For example, what would happen if you looked at the massive traffic jam you might find yourself in as a chance to listen to a book or foreign language program on tape? If you could *SHIFT* your perspective, you would in effect transform the event from a highly annoying pain in the neck to a bit of entertainment or a personal development session. Consider the impact if you *SHIFT* your mindset about the customer who just moved her business to your competitor. When you think about it, you realize that account required a lot of work for nominal profit. With that customer out of the picture, your time is freed up to attract new business or to up-sell existing accounts with higher margins. *When you change the way you look at things, things change.*

When we get hit with POWs, we often make them worse by obsessing about them. We "awfulize" the circumstances, letting our thoughts rule the day and imagining a disastrous ending to the stories of our life. This is what I call Fly Away Thinking™ – the self-made "tornado" in our brain that takes innocuous circumstances and turns them into whirling dervishes of fear, anxiety and frustration. It's the out-of-control, ever-faster-spinning spiral of negative thoughts that causes volatile emotions and knee-jerk reactions.

Funnel Thinking™, on the other hand, is taking charge of negative, unrestrained thoughts and focusing them into a more productive mindset. You create a mental "funnel" that eliminates pessimistic, unconstructive thoughts and pulls in the ones that are advantageous and constructive. As the name implies, Funnel Thinking forces you to carefully choose and allow into your mind only those specific thoughts that lead to a WOW.

Let's put these two ideas into context. Imagine that you arrive at work tomorrow to discover that your boss – whom you really enjoy working for – is leaving the company for a new job. Your initial response is "Congratulations!" Then reality sets in! You begin to wonder, "Oh no…how will this affect me?" and negative thoughts flood your mind. But the truth is that you don't know how this "story" will end. You have two options for finishing it. One is to let your Fly Away Thinking generate a less-than-pleasant ending to the situation. The other is to use Funnel Thinking to create an entirely different outcome. Let's take a look:

Fly Away Thinking	Funnel Thinking
✓ This will change everything! Why does bad stuff always happen to me?	✓ My boss has resigned and is leaving in three weeks. I'd better learn all I can before she leaves.
✓ This is our second new boss in two years! I knew it wouldn't last.	✓ This is just one more chance to change and grow.
✓ I was so happy with my boss. What if the new boss isn't as good as my boss now?	✓ The new boss could be even better, and I might enjoy working with him even more.
✓ What if they promote one of my coworkers?	✓ Senior management did a great job when they hired my current boss. They'll do a good job again.
✓ I bet this will cause turmoil and chaos around the office!	✓ My boss's boss is supportive of our department. I'm sure the transition will be smooth.
✓ I'd never be considered for the job even if I wanted it.	✓ I enjoy working for this company, and I'm doing well in my job.
✓ I can't think about work right now.	✓ I have work to do now.

Notice how Funnel Thinking fills your tank and gives you more energy, while Fly Away Thinking is an energy guzzler and drains you. Doesn't it make much more sense to simply keep your thoughts focused on what you know as of today instead of letting your thoughts spiral out of control? Don't jump to conclusions, make assumptions or worry about something that *might* happen in the future.

If you just can't help wondering about things to come, then at least be an optimist. I always say, **"If you don't know the ending to a story, then why not create a happy one?"** Before you start worrying about all the bad things that could happen, spend time envisioning the "happily ever after" version of the situation.

Mastering your thoughts is one of the most important principles you can learn. Identify them as harmful or helpful. Pay attention to the assumptions you make – are they mostly negative or positive? Notice how you tend to envision the future – is it with a lot of "what if…" scenarios? Much of the time, your mindset is the only thing that remains negative long after a situation is over. Are you ready to let go of your Fly Away Thinking and try a new thought pattern?

SHIFT Your Actions

Many people believe the secret to creating desired outcomes is simply to think positive thoughts. I believe it takes more than wishful thinking to change your reality – it takes action! The action corollary to Wayne Dyer's thought principle comes from Robert Collier, author of *The Secret of the Ages*: "If you don't make things happen, then things will happen to you." You can't simply sit back and think. You also have to *do* something in order to produce positive results.

Imagine you're going to host a special dinner party for friends. Your first step is to think through the guest list and envision the invitations. You mull over the decorations, picturing the table in your mind. You research recipes and create an impressive menu. Sounds like a great party! But what if you were to stop right there – at the thinking stage? When your guests arrived, you could tell them all about the beautiful decorations and the delicious menu, but you wouldn't have any food to serve them. This wouldn't be a dinner party; it would be a big tease! Your guests would literally be hungry for more. Get the picture?

To get to Professional Paradise, you must *SHIFT* your actions as well as your mindset. Many actions – especially those that occur in response to POWs – are spontaneous, without much thought as to the consequences. Although these automatic reactions can be helpful – like yanking your hand away from a hot stove – much of the time they do more harm than good. They tend to be impulsive, sometimes irrational and typically all-too-hasty. Add to that the fact that they're often counterproductive and prevent positive connections with others, and you can see why you want to *SHIFT*.

The trick to finding WOWs at work is to **intentionally choose your actions after *objectively* assessing the circumstances**. Thoughts are the first step, but it takes purposeful, constructive and intentional action to get to WOW.

Now let's put it all together to show how *SHIFT*ing your mindset and your actions can move you from Prison to Paradise. I'll use a recent incident to illustrate: I've been having problems with my cell phone dropping calls. When I'm on the road and need to be in contact with my clients, if my phone isn't working properly, it's a big POW. So I decided to call the technical support line at my wireless company for help. I'm going to share two different versions of how that call might have transpired. You decide which one seems more like a WOW.

Scenario #1:
As I looked for the toll-free number, I remembered the last few times I called the support line – things hadn't gone well. I was

already aggravated because I had a lot to do and this call would probably take 20 minutes that I didn't have.

I dialed the phone, a little edge in my attitude already. Of course, I got the ever annoying automated attendant which told me I needed to listen to the choices because they'd recently changed. Yeah, right! Do they really think people have memorized their choices? I selected technical support, and after a few rings I heard, "All of our agents are currently busy assisting other customers…we appreciate your patience." (Obviously they don't know how impatient I am.)

My jaw was clenched; my pulse sped up. The on-hold music was interfering with the tunes playing in my office. If only I could've delegated this to someone else. Why me? Why did my cell phone have to have problems? This was such a pain! I was ready to give the tech support person a piece of my mind….

I'll stop right there because I'm assuming you've lived through a similar experience and can guess how the rest of the call went. Now, the other version:

Scenario #2:
As I looked for the toll-free number, I remembered the last few times I called the support line – things hadn't gone well. I decided to be prepared for a long wait, so I grabbed a proposal I'd been working on. I couldn't afford to sit idly with all the work I had to do.

I dialed the phone, and of course, I got the ever annoying automated attendant, which told me I needed to listen to the choices because they'd recently changed. I laughed as I wondered out loud, "Who keeps changing these choices and why?" I selected technical support and heard, "All of our agents are currently busy assisting other customers…we appreciate your patience." I was ready for this. I lowered the volume on my headset (so the on-hold music wouldn't interfere with the tunes playing in my office) and got busy reviewing the proposal. Focusing on my work, I lost track of the time, and before I knew it a tech support person came on the line. I was calm and ready to talk about the issue and get it resolved.

Once again, I'll stop there. You probably have a good idea how that call ended. Here is my question for you: What stayed the same between the two scenarios and what changed?

What stayed the same?	What changed?
✓ I had a lot to do.	✓ I had a proposal ready to work on.
✓ I got the automated attendant.	✓ I laughed at the automated attendant.
✓ I was put on hold.	✓ I made good use of the wait time.
✓ I spoke with a technical support person.	✓ I was calm and level-headed when I spoke with the support person.

Basically, the event itself – the mechanics of the call – stayed the same. What changed was my mindset and therefore my actions. The big difference in the second version was my non-emotional, objective viewpoint about the experience. I bet you're wondering which of the two scenarios actually happened. If you guessed the second, you're correct. I did start with Fly Away Thinking that led down a negative path, but I caught myself, *SHIFT*ed and enjoyed the second experience.

Here's another true-life story of someone who *SHIFT*ed her mindset and her actions to transform a POW to a WOW: Roxanne is an associate at a large plant nursery. Recently, one of her coworkers totally re-created a display that Roxanne had spent hours working on. At one point in her life, Roxanne would have stormed up to the other employee and loudly confronted her about her actions. But after a while she realized that this approach wasn't getting good results (as you might imagine).

Once she learned to *SHIFT*, Roxanne recognized that her coworker wasn't trying to torture her, nor was she out to get her or "one up" her with the displays. Instead, the coworker was simply trying to make a positive contribution to the organization and was unaware how much her "touch ups" upset Roxanne. Using the *SHIFT* technique, Roxanne talked with her coworker about the incident, but in a way that enhanced their relationship instead of strained it. Note once again that the situation didn't change – Roxanne's mindset and actions did. That's the power of *SHIFT!*

Einstein's definition of insanity is often quoted: "Doing the same thing over and over again and expecting different results." If you're as smart as Einstein, you'll choose to *SHIFT* your mindset and *SHIFT* your actions the next time you get hit with a POW.

The ultimate goal, of course, is not only to get to Professional Paradise, but to stay there permanently. That's where the final piece comes in – *SHIFT*ing your habits. Whether you realize it or not, you've developed habitual responses to the common POWs you experience. To live the good life at work long term, you have to eliminate those harmful habits and replace them with new, helpful habits that lead to WOWs. In other words, **you must create a habit of consistently *SHIFT*ing your POWs to WOWs.** We'll talk about how to do that a bit later in the book in Part III. For now, let's keep *SHIFT*ing!

SHIFT to WOW

~~~~~~~~~~~~~~~~~~~~~~~~~~~~~~~~~~

The 5 Steps to *SHIFT*

At last, I'm going to give you your Passport to Professional Paradise – the *SHIFT* technique. I will walk you through the five steps necessary to *SHIFT* any POW to a WOW. Then, I'll share three *SHIFT* Strategies that will show you exactly how to put the steps into practice. When you're done, you'll be well on your way to less stress, more energy and remarkable results at work.

What does *SHIFT* stand for?

 Stop and breathe.

 Harness harmful knee-jerk reactions.

 Identify and manage negative emotions.

 Find new options.

 Take one positive action.

Let's dive in and look at each step individually. Imagine that you've just experienced a POW. Take a minute to vividly remember one of the POWs you wrote down earlier. Now…

Stop and breathe.

This first step is pretty straightforward. Notice that you're feeling stress or anger. Then, actually say, "Stop!" If you're alone in your office or car, you can speak the word. But POWs often hit us at inopportune moments in the midst of a crowd. No worries. Simply say, "Stop!" loudly *inside your head*. When you think or say "Stop," the messages that are firing throughout the brain are literally interrupted, allowing you to replace them with calmer, more rational thoughts.

Then take a deep cleansing breath. You don't have to get in a yoga pose or take a giant breath that draws the attention of everyone around you. But you do want to capture the benefits of deep breathing. I know from my nursing training that deep breathing increases the concentration of oxygen in the blood and releases endorphins which promote relaxation. It also causes your brain to begin making alpha waves, the kind of brain waves that gently calm you down. This is exactly what you need when you've been hit with a POW.

Some POWs take you by surprise while others are more predictable. Making a deep breath a conscious process slows down your reactions and buys you time – time to collect yourself and decide if you want to continue down the path you are on or change directions. Fortunately, you have everything you need to execute this first step wherever you are – in the cubicle, in the boardroom, in the showroom, on the shop floor or in the car.

Harness harmful knee-jerk reactions.

When you go to the doctor for your annual physical, he or she checks your reflexes by tapping a little hammer just below your kneecap. Your leg should jerk forward automatically. (If it doesn't, something's up!) You don't decide to kick your leg up, it's an involuntary reaction by your nervous system. That's where the term "knee-jerk reaction" came from, and now, it commonly means something you do automatically without thinking.

Knee-jerk reactions are our automatic, unthinking responses to POWs. The classic knee-jerk reaction that many people think of is the "fight or flight" response. Physiologically, humans are wired to either "put up their dukes" or "run for the hills" when challenged. In the days of the cavemen, this automatic reflex was very helpful when one was confronted by a hungry saber tooth tiger or a charging woolly mammoth. This knee-jerk reaction literally saved lives!

However, in today's business environment, fight or flight can get us into trouble. More objective thinking and different actions are usually far more effective. Fight or flight in response to a POW can range from storming out of the room to becoming a "shrinking violet." Other common knee-jerk reactions include taking things personally, sarcasm, raising your voice, complaining, sulking, talking fast, name calling, blaming others and talking about people behind their back.

If you are not *consciously* evaluating your thoughts in response to a POW, then you are letting knee-jerk reactions take charge. Negative knee-jerk reactions perpetuate, amplify and exaggerate the effects of a POW. Harnessing them keeps you from making a fool of yourself and gives you the chance to make conscious decisions and choices.

Learn to identify your knee-jerk reactions and determine if they are harmful or helpful. One of my big pet peeves is waiting in lines. I know that's a POW for me. When I see a line, I take a deep breath, unclench my hands (my knee-jerk reaction) and then look around to see how I can entertain myself while I wait. Knowing that I'm likely to get impatient in lines helps me keep my knee-jerk reactions in check.

In the heat of a POW, you may not feel like you can harness your knee-jerk reactions. But I'm here to tell you that, with practice, you will be able to. So, how do I do it? It's pretty simple. At the first sign of a negative knee-jerk reaction, (after I've taken my deep breath), I ask myself, **"Is (my reaction) going to improve the situation? Who will be most negatively affected by my reaction?"** Usually the answer is "me." I'm the one whose blood pressure is escalating, whose pulse is racing and who's starting to sweat. My knee-jerk reactions might be bothersome to others, but they are always more detrimental to me, and that's reason enough to stop!

Using *SHIFT* creates *positive* knee-jerk reactions rather than harmful ones. In the long run, negative responses create more stress, anxiety and trouble in your life. Everyone benefits when you harness your negative knee-jerk reactions, but you benefit the most.

*I*dentify and manage negative emotions.

According to Wikipedia.com, "emotion, in its most general definition, is a complex psychophysical process that arises spontaneously, rather than through conscious effort." It goes on to say that emotion "evokes either a positive or negative psychological response and physical expressions, often involuntary, related to feelings, perceptions or beliefs…in reality or in the imagination." Sounds kind of complex and scientific, doesn't it? Put more simply, **our emotional response to a POW causes our knee-jerk reaction**. But in terms of *SHIFT*ing the pattern, we must first stop the knee-jerk reaction. Once we've harnessed that, then we're in a position to identify and manage the emotions behind it.

The first part of "I" is to identify the negative emotions you're experiencing. That means you have to make a conscious effort to notice where in your body you feel these emotions and then name them. I feel anxiety as a queasy stomach; someone else might feel it as a headache. Each of us experiences emotions differently, so the key is to know yourself.

The second part of this step is to manage the negative emotions. Once you know which emotions you're dealing with, you can choose to break the pattern. Have you ever been in an argument with someone where voices were raised and emotions were running high – and then the phone rang? One of you stopped to answer the phone, and the caller was greeted with a sunny "hello." It's like a switch was flipped. The person who answered the phone was still angry but was able to temporarily put his or her emotions on hold.

That's what I mean by short-term management of negative emotions. This step is about learning how to flip the switch (in a helpful way) on your emotions to put you on the road from POW to WOW. I'm not recommending that you turn them off or shove them under the rug. I'm suggesting that you *manage* them so that you can proceed – consciously – in a positive direction. Talk to yourself in a calm rational manner such as, "I'm not going to get worked up over this" or "I don't know what's going on, so I'm going to assume it will end positively."

Another great way to flip the switch is to gain some perspective. What difference, *truly*, does it (the POW) make? And more importantly, what good will it do you to continue with the negative emotions? Let's say you receive a report from a colleague that contains a few errors. Instead of taking it personally or feeling frustrated and upset, put the situation in the proper perspective. "Okay, so there are a couple of mistakes. I know this person worked hard on this. It will take me ten minutes max to correct them. This is no big deal."

Understand that I'm not going all "Dr. Phil" here. I'm not talking about an in-depth analysis of your deep-seated emotions and fears. I'm simply pointing out that it's a good idea to identify and manage your negative emotions because the person they hurt the most is *you*.

*F*ind new options.

This step puts you in a proactive position instead of a reactive one. When you take a few minutes to consider new options, you move closer to WOW and closer to Professional Paradise. The void of the negative knee-jerk reaction can be filled with the excitement of fresh ideas. Having choices provides a feeling of being in control, which most people appreciate. Being creative and thinking of a variety of options opens up possibilities that may have gone unnoticed in the past.

When considering new options (by "new" I mean an approach that's different than the one you might typically use), of course you want to think about specific action steps that will get you to WOW. I invoke the "Rule of Three" to find new options:

1. *What has worked in the past?* Think about another time when you were hit with this particular POW and remember what worked. For example, when a customer complains, think back to a customer with a similar problem whom you were able to make happy, and try that option.

2. *What would someone you admire do?* Think of someone you know personally or respect from a distance and figure out what s/he would do in a similar situation. I have a small sign that says "What would Gandhi do?" on my refrigerator. This is a helpful reminder when I'm hit with a POW at home.

Ask yourself, "What would (<u>my boss, my best friend, my brother, someone really patient, etc.</u>) do?"

3. *What would someone objective do?* This third tactic builds on the first two. What if you were observing this situation from an outsider's perspective? All too often we take things personally when they aren't personal at all. Put yourself in the shoes of an onlooker and see what options appear. From a distance, things often seem funny, light hearted or even ridiculous (if you engage your sense of humor).

Remember, there is *always* more than one way to complete a task or solve a problem. Try the Rule of Three to find new options, and you'll be well on your way to Professional Paradise.

*T*ake one positive action.

Once you've discovered new possibilities, the final step is to choose at least one that feels right for the situation and **take action!** This is the action part of *SHIFT*. It takes what was merely positive thinking and moves it toward reality. Remember, thoughts alone rarely achieve anything. You must act if you want a better outcome.

MINDSET ⟶ ACTIONS ⟶ OUTCOMES

You can certainly choose to implement more than one option, but one is the minimum needed to create a true *SHIFT*. Which option will produce the best results? Which one will get you one step closer to less stress, more energy and remarkable results? Which one will create the biggest WOW? Once you decide…take action!

That's it! Those are the five steps to *SHIFT* any POW to a WOW. Using this technique, you can transform virtually any negative or unpleasant situation into one that's not only tolerable, but also productive and beneficial. Here's a real-life example that illustrates all five *SHIFT* steps and will put the puzzle together for you.

It had been a long day. I was on the tarmac in a crowded airplane in Charlotte, NC, and we were next in line for takeoff. Many flights to destinations north of Baltimore, MD, (my hometown) had been cancelled or delayed due to bad weather, but it seemed like we would be okay. Only one hour until I'd be back in Baltimore driving home to my family.

And then the pilot came on the overhead speaker and said, "I was afraid it was too good to be true. We're being asked to stay here and wait while air traffic in the Baltimore area clears out. We're going to park the plane out here and shut off one of the engines to save fuel. I'll update you as soon as I know anything more." *POW!*

I needed to *SHIFT* from POW to WOW. Here's exactly what I did on that plane:

Stop and breathe. I firmly thought, "Stop!" and then reminded myself to breathe. I leaned back in my seat, closed my eyes, unclenched my fists and took several deep breaths.

Harness harmful knee-jerk reactions. My initial reaction was to start complaining to the people sitting around me. (Funny – that also seemed to be the reaction of just about everyone else on board.) I also had a strong desire to jump up, run screaming toward the nearest exit and get off the plane! However, I recognized that these knee-jerk reactions were neither practical nor helpful. I harnessed them before I caused myself more stress.

Identify and manage negative emotions. I took note of my sweaty palms and queasy stomach. I acknowledged that I was feeling frustration, aggravation and, yes, some anxiety about the possibility of not getting home. Fortunately, I quickly realized that dwelling on these negative feelings was not going to clear out the skies above Baltimore or get our plane off the tarmac any faster. I chose to put things in perspective – in the scheme of my life, or even my week, was this really a big deal, even if I had to spend one night sleeping in a chair at the airport? No, it wasn't.

*F*ind new options. I tried to think of a few constructive or relaxing things I could do while we sat and waited. But I didn't want to read the magazine in the seat pocket, and I wasn't sleepy. What else was there to do? I decided to use the Rule of Three and thought of my friend Ed, a world-class business traveler. I wondered, "What would Ed do?" I figured he might catch up on some work, listen to some music (he has a great iPod collection), make a few phone calls or read.

*T*ake one positive action. In this case, I decided that the music would be a great option – it's a wonderful stress reducer for me. My music selection is upbeat and always puts me in a good mood. So out came the iPod. I also decided to read a book which was a very pleasurable way to pass the time. I had successfully *SHIFT*ed a POW to a WOW.

Luckily, our delay was only about 20 minutes. However, we ended up circling over Baltimore for a while and then sitting on the tarmac there for close to an hour before we could get to our gate. But I had my *SHIFT* steps in place by then. What could have really felt like being trapped in Prison instead turned into a little slice of Paradise.

You might be wondering when to use *SHIFT*. I use it all the time – whenever something starts to create stress in my life – whether I've caused the problem or someone else has. You can use *SHIFT* for coping with big, highly stressful events like a surprise layoff or some tragic office event. And you can also use it for everyday nuisances such as a printer breakdown, having to reschedule a meeting or an offhanded comment by a colleague.

After I developed the *SHIFT* technique and began using it, I quickly realized that it's effective in all different types of work (and personal) situations. However, I also observed some common themes. The *SHIFT* technique tends to fall into three main categories of use at work:

✦ **Viewpoint*SHIFT*** – Producing better outcomes in tough situations

✦ **Connection*SHIFT*** – Creating positive relationships with coworkers and customers

✦ **Solution*SHIFT*** – Finding the best solutions to your most challenging problems

Let's learn more about each of these and practice using them to *SHIFT* your POWs to WOWs.

Viewpoint*SHIFT*

Producing better outcomes in tough situations

Do you get defensive or take things personally? **POW!**

Ever assume something without having all the facts and then realize you made a mistake? **POW!**

Do you overreact to minor issues that just don't matter in the scheme of things? **POW!**

If you answered "Yes" to any of these questions, then a Viewpoint*SHIFT* is just what you need to turn those POWs into WOWs.

Are you familiar with the hit song "I Can See Clearly Now" that was written and recorded by Johnny Nash in the 1970s? Here are just a few lines of the lyrics:

I can see clearly now the rain is gone
I can see all obstacles in my way.
Gone are the dark clouds that had me blind.
It's gonna be a bright (bright), bright (bright) sunshiny day.

I like that song because it reminds me of a Viewpoint*SHIFT*. You see, a Viewpoint*SHIFT* clears away misconceptions you may have about certain situations and allows you to see events and people more objectively. It shines light on the situation, so to speak. As a result, you become more adaptable and open minded – you see things more clearly. A Viewpoint*SHIFT* will help you systematically change your mindset and your actions in order to reduce your stress and create more energy in any difficult situation.

According to *The American Heritage Dictionary*, viewpoint means "a [mental] position from which something is observed or considered." Your viewpoint is the lens through which you see the world. It influences every experience you have and every action you take. One person sees the glass as half empty; another sees it as half full.

Have you noticed that when you complain or are unhappy at work, it often has to do with your internal thoughts (specifically your viewpoint or mindset) about the situation and not necessarily the event itself? Suppose a customer sends you an email asking you to contact her later in the day. All of a sudden, you assume the worst and become consumed with worry. Instead of focusing on other work, you create all sorts of negative scenarios in your mind, none of which have a happy ending. It's not the email that creates the drama; it's your viewpoint about the email that causes all the trouble. The customer might want to give you good news – perhaps he's referred a colleague to you. Sometimes a pessimistic viewpoint keeps us trapped in Professional Prison or on Parole because we create obstacles in our minds that don't exist in reality.

How often do people in the workplace have different viewpoints? *All* the time. Usually that's a good thing. Different viewpoints unleash fresh, creative solutions and can produce impressive results. But differing viewpoints can also become roadblocks to remarkable results and create great strife and stress in the work environment. Think about a typical office on a typical day with a typical team. With 10 or 15 people on the team, there are countless opportunities for differing viewpoints about many situations. Add in other departments, leaders, customers and suppliers, and you have literally hundreds of chances for conflict and clashes to erupt. I believe that people often become defensive when someone disagrees with their viewpoint because they assume they are being personally attacked. So, they tend to fight back instead of listening to the other person's concerns and considering that another perspective might be valid.

A Viewpoint*SHIFT* is crucial whenever you need **perspective**... when you:

- ✦ Feel defensive or take things personally;

- ✦ Make a mountain out of a molehill and get worked up over a situation that doesn't matter when you look at the big picture;

- ✦ Don't like how someone is doing something and you can't seem to let it go;

- ✦ Worry about things that haven't even happened yet;

- ✦ Overstep your bounds and get involved in someone else's business;

- ✦ Make assumptions without having all the information.

Each of these signs is a clue that your mindset is more than likely contributing to your POWs. Has your outlook ever gotten in the way of creating positive connections with coworkers or producing remarkable results? Take a few minutes right now to think about a time when your viewpoint alone was the cause of your problem.

The great news is that with a Viewpoint*SHIFT*, you can change your perspective and create more WOWs. According to Zen

Buddhists, when you have a Beginner's Mind you see many possibilities, you lack preconceptions and your outlook is broad and deep. On the other hand, those with an Expert's Mind often have limiting views which shrink their viewpoint. Isn't that interesting? You would think you'd want an Expert's Mind, when in reality the Beginner's Mind is more beneficial. A Viewpoint*SHIFT* helps you foster a Beginner's Mind.

Now let's take a look at a Viewpoint*SHIFT* in a real work-related situation. Rosalie is a manager in the Human Resources (HR) department of a mid-sized company. She oversees benefits administration and her "customers" are the employees of the organization. Rosalie and her staff recently orchestrated a conversion to a new software system that automated many of the functions they used to do by hand. As a result, employees can now go online 24-7 for benefits information instead of calling the HR department during business hours.

Rosalie was sitting at her desk working when an employee just walked into her office. She'd seen him around, but didn't know his name. He walked right up to her desk and, before she could get a word out, said "I'm Maurice from the Production Department. I'm here to tell you that I don't appreciate what you've done. It's ridiculous that we have to go online to check benefits. Not everyone sits in front of a computer all day, you know. If you don't do something to fix this right now, I'm going to go to my boss and complain." ***POW!***

Rosalie immediately became defensive. She stood up behind her desk. "I beg your pardon?" she retorted. "You can't just barge in here and tell me how to do my job!" She was seething inside. "Who does he think he is?" she thought. Who was this guy to question her judgment? He had no idea how carefully she and her staff had worked to make sure the new system was easy to use. What nerve!

Now, I'll walk you through the five steps of a ViewpointSHIFT that Rosalie used to change her POW to a WOW.

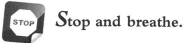

Stop and breathe.

Rosalie was definitely worked up. But she prides herself on maintaining her professionalism. She feels that as an HR leader it's her job to role-model positive behavior. She decided she'd better get back in control. "I've got to stop and calm down," she thought. She invited Maurice to sit down and then took a deep breath as she sat back down.

Harness harmful knee-jerk reactions.

Typical knee-jerk reactions when you need a ViewpointSHIFT include lashing out at others, automatically assuming you know what's going on, raising your voice, presuming the worst-case scenario, not giving others a chance to express their opinions, and thinking others are out to get you.

Rosalie's knee-jerk reaction was to defend herself from the perceived attack. Her automatic fight response kicked in, and she stood up and lashed out at Maurice. Fortunately, she caught herself and thought, "This isn't appropriate. Plus, getting mad isn't going to help anything." She quickly apologized to Maurice and suggested they start over.

Identify and manage negative emotions.

Common negative emotions when your viewpoint is out of whack include defensiveness, resentment, exasperation, resistance to change, concern and cynicism. Rosalie initially felt attacked. She resented

Maurice for questioning her decision-making process, and she was offended by his remarks and his threat to go to his boss. This whole transition hadn't even been her idea – it was forced on her to begin with! She recognized all the negative feelings that were welling up. She stopped the Fly Away Thinking and made a conscious effort to engage in Funnel Thinking.

*F*ind new options.

Rosalie reminded herself that her goal was to serve the employees and to adequately address their concerns. She quickly ran through some options in her mind that would move both her and Maurice to WOW. The ideas Rosalie considered are the same options you can use for a Viewpoint*SHIFT*:

✦ Give yourself time and space to think things through before taking any action.

✦ Consciously choose to write a happy ending to the "story."

✦ Collect more data and get all the information before making assumptions, judgments or decisions.

✦ Quit taking it personally (QTIP).

✦ Let go of old grudges and hurt feelings.

✦ Assume others are acting with positive intent.

✦ Decide to be more open minded and genuinely listen to others' ideas and perspectives.

✦ Use the Rule of Three (what worked in the past, what would someone you admire do, what would someone objective do).

 ## *T*ake one positive action.

Rosalie realized she was taking Maurice's comments personally when they weren't personal at all. She decided it would be more productive to look at things from his viewpoint, so she began asking him questions in an effort to learn more. She wanted to be sure she clearly understood his concerns. As they talked, she began to appreciate that he was frustrated despite all of her hard work. After all, it wasn't that surprising that someone with limited computer access would be upset that he could no longer get his information personally. This new program wasn't going to please everyone – her team had discussed that very issue at the beginning of the project.

Do you agree with the options Rosalie chose? What would you have done? After talking with Maurice – and later, with other members of his department – Rosalie and her team encouraged employees who didn't have computer access at work to contact the HR department for their benefits information and questions. Since the vast majority of employees had computers, the new system greatly reduced her team's workload. They were more than happy to continue to personally serve those employees who called in. Now that's a **WOW** – for everyone!

Some of you may be thinking, "Why did Rosalie have to change her viewpoint? Why didn't Maurice change his?" Ideally, everyone involved in a situation should engage in a Viewpoint*SHIFT* in order to create the best outcome. But in reality, the only viewpoint you can change is your own. You can be stubborn and say, "If others won't change their viewpoint, then I'm not going to change mine," or you can step up and own your half of the interaction and get much better results.

That is exactly what is so fantastic about a Viewpoint*SHIFT* – **you can change the whole tenor of a situation by simply changing your viewpoint.** Your ability to be flexible and open-minded provides endless possibilities for resolving conflicts to your satisfaction and living the good life at work.

What will it be: a victim viewpoint or a Viewpoint*SHIFT*? The choice is yours!

*Letting go of your own biases and judgments...**WOW!***

*Walking in someone else's shoes...**WOW!***

*Seeing things for what they are – no big deal...**WOW!***

ViewpointSHIFT Exercise

This is your chance to apply what you've learned and a valuable step in creating a *SHIFT* habit. You may be thinking, "I don't want to do this exercise," but I assure you that practicing and personalizing the steps are crucial to making them work for you! (To download a free 8.5" x 11" version of this exercise, go to www.ProfessionalParadise.com.)

1. Under "POW," give a brief description of a recent situation where you felt defensive or believed you were the victim, blamed, wronged, etc., including your viewpoint of the situation.

2. Under "S" write the word STOP. (This will help you remember to say "Stop!" and breathe the next time you're hit with a POW.)

3. Under "H" list the harmful knee-jerk reactions you had in response to the POW you described in Step 1.

4. Under "I" list the negative emotions you experienced.

5. Under "F" list as many ideas as you can think of that are new options for the scenario you described.

6. Under "T" write down at least one action you will take if you are faced with this POW again.

7. Under "WOW" list the positive outcomes that would result from this ViewpointSHIFT.

POW	Stop and breathe	Harness knee-jerk reactions	Identify & manage negative emotions	Find new options	Take one positive action	WOW

Connection*SHIFT*

~~~~~~~~~~~~~~~~~~~~

Creating positive relationships with coworkers and customers

Coworkers getting on your nerves? **POW!**

Got cranky customers you'd like to avoid? **POW!**

Don't see eye to eye with your boss or direct report? **POW!**

In my own research with more than one thousand people, when asked what makes them happy at work, a full 42 percent cited positive interactions with other people as the most important factor in workplace satisfaction. These interactions included creating connections with coworkers and customers, receiving appreciation from others, working effectively on teams and demonstrating care and concern for others. In addition, numerous studies have shown that the quality of an individual's relationship with his or her immediate leader is the most significant factor in turnover and retention. In other words, your connection (or lack thereof) with your boss is a significant factor in the quality of your work experience.

A Connection*SHIFT* is a tool for turning relationship POWs into WOWs. It creates a positive association between people. The intentional act of establishing a connection with someone in order to better understand their position is a living example of the words of St. Francis of Assisi (made popular in modern times by Stephen Covey): "Grant that I may not so much seek to be understood as to understand."

At the most basic level, a connection occurs when two or more things are joined together. Connections are at the heart of business, because little gets done without some degree of interaction or joining together with others. Think about it: Organizations must connect with their customers, their suppliers and their shareholders. Departments must connect with one another in order to deliver products and services – production with procurement, marketing with sales, customer service with fulfillment. **Without connections, there is no business, no commerce**. Read that again and let the full impact of its truth sink in.

Ultimately, all of these interactions come down to individuals – people like you and me – connecting with each other on a personal basis. Who do you have to connect with in order to get your job done – coworkers, teammates, leaders, colleagues in other departments, customers, vendors? Which connections are positive and which ones *aren't but should be*? Remember, you don't have to be fast friends with everyone. You just need to work with them when the need arises.

Unfortunately, workplace connections are a primary source of POWs for most people. Because there are so many factors that affect relationships, there are lots of things that can go wrong. Let's look at some common causes of relationship POWs.

Interpersonal disconnects are often the result of conflicting work beliefs. Think back to the belief chapter and all the things that go into the belief system that drives our thoughts and actions on the job. It's easy to see how connections can be hindered or damaged when our work beliefs conflict with others' beliefs.

Bad first impressions make for a lot of relationship POWs. Consciously or unconsciously, we all form first impressions that directly influence our desire and willingness to connect with others. Customer service experts tell us that you have only six seconds to make a great first impression. That's fast! So in the first few seconds you meet someone, talk to them on the phone or read an email from them, you are deciding how you will connect with them – and they with you! Allowing a negative first impression to hinder a connection is definitely a knee-jerk reaction – one that can be hard to overcome.

A final reason for weak connections is the way we communicate these days. In an electronic world, it's far too easy for people to avoid face-to-face interactions. As a result, connections between people become muddled (if they exist at all). Even though they work in the same building or on the same floor, people use email to address tough issues, avoid confrontation and cover their back side. This use of technology almost always backfires because there's simply too much room for misinterpretation.

Whew! It's no wonder people aren't connecting!

Thank goodness you have the Connection*SHIFT* strategy in your toolbox. Use it anytime you want to create a strong link with others:

- ✦ Meeting with a prospect to pitch new business;
- ✦ Completing inter-departmental projects;
- ✦ Dealing with unhappy customers;
- ✦ Working with your boss or direct reports;
- ✦ Networking with colleagues outside the office;
- ✦ Collaborating on a team project.

A Connection*SHIFT* will help you get along better with others. But I'm not suggesting that you roll over and take it when conflicts arise or people upset you. In fact, I'm suggesting the opposite. A Connection*SHIFT* allows you to "speak your truth" in a way that others are able to hear. It's one thing to tell a coworker in a respectful manner that you're disappointed about something he did; it's quite another to blame, complain and accuse him. See the difference? You speak your truth in both instances, but using *SHIFT* creates a relationship WOW instead of a relationship POW. A Connection*SHIFT* also helps you remain calm and objective so you can hear other people's "truths" behind the noise of their defensiveness, knee-jerk reactions and negative emotions.

There are many reasons to make the effort to create positive connections with everyone you interact with at work. Connection WOWs lead to a less stressful, more peaceful workplace. Sounds good, doesn't it? But I want to make certain you understand that this is much more than "feel good" stuff (although I'm not sure why feeling good isn't a big enough benefit for us all!).

There are many tangible benefits to *SHIFT*ing relationship POWs to WOWs. As an individual, you're *guaranteed* to get your work done more easily, more quickly and with better results. Let me say that again. You are guaranteed to get your work done more easily, more quickly and with better results. Compare a day spent butting heads to one with positive connections, and you'll know exactly what I mean. For the organization, connection WOWs translate to less overtime, increased efficiency and productivity, more sales and a better bottom line. Oh yeah, and one more: happier customers (which leads to repeat business and referrals)!

Let's see how a Connection*SHIFT* works in the real world. The story takes place in a small community hospital. Our cast of characters includes Kimi, a 28-year-old registered nurse in charge of her unit, and Michelle, a 48-year-old veteran pharmacist. Kimi is exasperated by pharmacy orders that are consistently late. She's had several phone conversations with Michelle and feels that Michelle isn't on board with the new technology the hospital purchased. Now another medication order is missing, and Kimi is certain Michelle has purposely delayed it just to spite her.

Kimi needs a Connection*SHIFT* in the worst way!

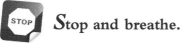 **S**top and breathe.

When Kimi got the news about the missing medication from a fellow nurse, she started to lose her temper. "Stop!" she said to herself and took a deep breath to calm her nerves.

Harness harmful knee-jerk reactions.

Typical knee-jerk reactions for connection snafus include being critical or defensive, gossiping, making inappropriate comments, exhibiting negative body language or voice tone, blaming, being confrontational, walking away, mentally shutting down or not accepting responsibility. Poor customer connections can cause employees to complain, pass the customer off to others, have a negative attitude, or do sloppy work.

Kimi's immediate reaction was to call the nursing manager to complain about the pharmacy problems. She also would've loved to have stormed down to the pharmacy and had a blunt conversation with Michelle. Instead, she harnessed her reactions and went to the break room to cool off.

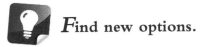 ### *I*dentify and manage negative emotions.

Connection POWs might cause you to feel isolated, irritated, annoyed, disliked, unkind, threatened, picked on or singled out. Since connections always involve two or more people, remember to also consider the possible negative emotions of the others involved.

Kimi acknowledged her frustration. This was stressful. Late medications created lots of problems with physicians, for her unit and for her patients. She knew she had to connect with Michelle to resolve this issue once and for all.

*F*ind new options.

Here are several options Kimi – and you – can use to make a Connection*SHIFT*:

+ Practice *Swan Seeking*™ – find at least one good thing about the other person.

+ Ask others questions to learn more about what's happening with them (seek first to understand) and carefully listen to what they say.

+ Rehearse your lines before any kind of conversation to make sure they are positive.

+ Envision a strong connection in advance of a meeting or interaction.

+ State that you want to create a positive connection with the other people involved.

+ Apologize for any hard feelings that arose as a result of a misunderstanding.

+ Use the Rule of Three (what worked in the past, what would someone you admire do, what would someone objective do).

Do you remember the story "The Ugly Duckling" by Hans Christian Andersen? The ugly duckling hatched among a group of ducks who did not take kindly to his odd looks. So he left and went looking for a place where he fit in. Eventually, he found other animals who accepted him for what he was — a swan. He'd been a swan all along, but none of the other animals had seen his potential. All too often we only see the ugly ducklings in others, when in fact they are beautiful swans. And the way we see others has a direct impact on our relationships. Which do you look for in others — the ugly duckling or the swan? They are one and the same. The only thing that changes is your mindset.

Make a choice to look for the good in people — to do some "Swan Seeking." When a negative trait pops into your mind, work to create a positive connection instead. There is good in everyone; you just have to find it. If you did nothing other than Swan Seeking, you'd turn many of your relationship POWs into WOWs, and you'd be much closer to living the good life at work.

Kimi realized it wasn't reasonable for her to assume Michelle had done this on purpose. Although Michelle was aloof and seemed a bit smug, Kimi had to admit she was the consummate professional (Swan Seeking). Michelle would never intentionally hold up a medication. Perhaps she needed to visit the pharmacy and talk with Michelle to find out more information.

 *T*ake one positive action.

Kimi calmly headed to the pharmacy. When she arrived she said to Michelle, "Do you have a minute to talk about the pharmacy orders on my unit? I know we've had some problems, and this will give us a chance to iron out some things that might be getting in the way." Kimi asked some questions and learned about some challenges the pharmacy had been having with the new software. In the end, they both realized they experienced similar challenges at work, and they felt better about their relationship.

I bet I know what you're thinking: "But you haven't met my boss or my coworkers. They are impossible to get along with!" The Connection*SHIFT* strategy works with all kinds of people, even the most challenging ones. You might just have to be a little more patient and a little more assertive with a really tough connection. (If you need detailed information about dealing with difficult people, check out the *Bullies, Babies & Brats: Get Along with Anyone at Work* audio CD at www.VickiHess.com.)

What will it be – a connection shambles or a Connection*SHIFT*? The choice is yours…starting today.

Listening without interrupting… ***WOW!***

Connecting with your boss more effectively
so that she accepts and values your input… ***WOW!***

Taking the time to learn more about a difficult customer's interests
and hobbies, and really enjoying yourself… ***WOW!***

Connection*SHIFT* Exercise

This is your chance to apply what you've learned and a valuable step in creating a *SHIFT* habit. You may be thinking, "I don't want to do this exercise," but I assure you that practicing and personalizing the steps are crucial to making them work for you! (To download a free 8.5" x 11" version of this exercise, go to www.ProfessionalParadise.com.)

1. Under "POW," give a brief description of a recent meeting or conversation you had with a coworker or customer that created a negative connection, including why you were having a tough time connecting positively.

2. Under "S," write the word STOP. (This will help you remember to say "Stop!" and breathe the next time you're hit with a POW.)

3. Under "H" list the harmful knee-jerk reactions you had in response to the POW you described in Step 1.

4. Under "I" list the negative emotions you experienced.

5. Under "F" list as many ideas as you can think of that are new options for the scenario you described.

6. Under "T" write down at least one action you will take if you are faced with this POW again.

7. Under "WOW" list the positive outcomes that would result from this Connection*SHIFT*.

POW	Stop and breathe	Harness knee-jerk reactions	Identify & manage negative emotions	Find new options	Take one positive action	WOW

Solution*SHIFT*

~~~~~~~~~~~~~~~~~~~~~~~

Finding the best solutions to your most challenging problems

Ever disagree with someone about the best way to complete a task or project? **POW!**

Do you get frustrated or stuck when you can't solve a problem on the first try? **POW!**

Tired of being right but not happy? **POW!**

Most people spend a great deal of their time at work solving problems. Stop and think for a minute about your typical day. Isn't problem solving in some form or fashion much of what you do? You might be solving problems for a customer, your boss, direct report, another department or another team member. Or perhaps you deal with technology snafus, time-management challenges or leadership problems.

In my experience, problem solving is also one of the most difficult (and ultimately satisfying) tasks we face at work. Why? Because very few problems involve black-and-white issues, and there isn't one proven method for solving every challenge or dilemma that arises.

Problem solving is also challenging, I believe, because humans have a powerful need to be right. I've studied people in solution-seeking mode for years, and I've observed this time and time again. Do *you* have a strong need to be right? (Be honest!) If so, why?

A Solution*SHIFT* is a potent problem-solving strategy. I'm sure you've heard the saying, "There are three sides to every story: your version, the other person's version and the truth." Likewise, there are three solutions to every problem: your solution, the other person's solution and the *best* solution. A Solution*SHIFT* guides you in objectively evaluating many possible answers – from both parties' perspectives. It allows you to let someone else be right without losing face and offers an opportunity to achieve the **best solution for the situation**. (By the way, "best for the situation" doesn't necessarily equate to a win/win solution.) Isn't that what you really want, after all?

A Solution*SHIFT* does not provide a win-at-all-costs or a give-in solution. Instead, it works within the framework of your objectives and helps you develop several solutions to find the most appropriate one for the given circumstances. It is especially powerful because it enables you to give up your emotional attachment to *your* solution so you can choose a more productive one. Who knows…you might learn to comfortably say, "I didn't think of that" or "I can learn something in this situation" or even the dreaded "I was wrong."

A Solution*SHIFT* comes in handy with all kinds of problems, conflicts and disagreements. Here are just a few examples of POWs that can be resolved with a Solution*SHIFT*:

- ✦ You and a coworker must resolve a product quality issue.
- ✦ A client wants you to lower your prices.
- ✦ Your supervisor gives you a new assignment that you think is unfair.

✦ You and a fellow team member "butt heads" about the best way to complete a task.

✦ Your customer is frustrated with a service issue that you have no control over.

Using a Solution*SHIFT* to transform problem POWs into solution WOWs will give you an ideal resolution plus contentment. And do you want to be right or be happy? Happy is so much more satisfying in the long run.

Let's see how a Solution*SHIFT* can take two professionals from POW to WOW. Anthony is a technician for an IT consulting firm. He works mostly onsite at client locations resolving technology-related issues. Estelle is the key contact at one of his biggest clients. She can be difficult at times, expecting Anthony to drop everything to come to her office whenever she calls. The support contract stipulates next-day service, but she expects a faster response. One day while working with another client, Anthony received a frantic voicemail from Estelle: "One of our busiest printers is down, and you need to get over here ASAP! If you can't get it fixed within the next few hours, you can kiss this account goodbye!" **POW!**

Anthony was sick and tired of Estelle throwing her weight around, and he wasn't in the mood to deal with her. He was fairly certain based on her description of the problem that fixing the printer would require getting a new part, which would take at least a day or two. His patience was hanging by a thread.

I'm going to use Anthony and Estelle's story to illustrate the steps of a Solution*SHIFT*:

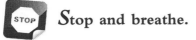 ## Stop and breathe.

Anthony realized that he was gunning for a fight and that he and Estelle were potentially headed for trouble. "Stop," he said. "I've got to take a minute and think this through." He stepped outside and took a deep breath.

Harness harmful knee-jerk reactions.

Typical knee-jerk reactions to problems and challenges include fighting for your solution, summarily rejecting others' solutions, trying to convince the other person that you're right and he/she is wrong, talking faster, giving up, giving in, and using negative body language such as folded or flailing arms. Watch people the next time you see a disagreement at work and notice the knee-jerk reactions that play out.

Knee-jerk reactions to customer-related problems tend to be more subtle and passive-aggressive since most people know better than to overtly aggravate their bread and butter. In the case of a stalemate with a client, you might talk to yourself, use sarcasm, say something acceptable but with closed body language, or deliberately not return phone calls or emails.

Anthony's natural response was to dig in to his position. He was, after all, "right" based on the stipulations in the service contract. Maybe he should make a copy of the contract, highlight the next-day service clause and show it to her. He hadn't even picked up the phone to call Estelle yet, but he could feel his blood pressure rising. "I'd better get a handle on myself or I could lose this account," he thought.

Identify and manage negative emotions.

Without a doubt, unresolved problems will stress you out and sap your energy. You could also feel disappointed, aggravated or intimidated. Or you might feel the need to "win" at all costs, be worried about what the other person thinks of you, or get agitated because you're not getting your way. You can better manage your emotions by making a concerted effort to focus on the *facts* of the problem at hand, not your *feelings* about the problem at hand.

Another critical element in a SolutionSHIFT is to think about *the other person's* negative emotions because they also play a key role in the problem-solving process. Notice what is going on with the other person. What do you think he or she might be feeling? Focusing on the other party is a great catalyst for being more objective.

When Anthony finally stopped thinking about how he was going to convince Estelle he was right and she was wrong, he was able to acknowledge his anger. And once he got that out of the way, he could see the problem more clearly. He also knew from past experiences that Estelle could be hot tempered and stubborn. Thinking through how she might be feeling and how she might react allowed him to better plan his approach with her.

Find new options.

A multitude of alternative options exist for a SolutionSHIFT. Some possibilities include:

+ Objectively describe the facts of the situation.
+ Acknowledge that there are many ways to "skin a cat" and accept that your solution might not be the best.
+ Identify at least one solution that hasn't been considered and request that the other person do the same.

◆ Let go of your ego and decide to be happy, not necessarily right.

◆ Once you've chosen the best solution for the situation, release your emotional attachment to your original ideas and say "thank you" to the other person.

◆ Actively listen with an open mind to the other person and his/her solution. Ask questions if necessary to clarify and improve your understanding of the idea.

◆ Agree to reach a consensus solution and commit to supporting it.

◆ Ask others to share their objections to your solution and respectfully consider ways to resolve their concerns.

◆ Agree to compromise.

◆ Use the Rule of Three (what worked in the past, what would someone you admire do, what would someone objective do).

Sometimes in a Solution*SHIFT* you simply have to liberate yourself from your ego, let go and move forward with someone else's solution. Ahhhh – that feels good. Then there are circumstances in which everyone agrees to listen objectively and come to a consensus. Sometimes you compromise – each person gives a little in hope of finding some common ground. And there are those times when you passionately believe in the merits of your solution. That's when you respectfully listen to others' concerns about your idea and develop creative ways to resolve them.

When seeking a Solution*SHIFT*, steer away from absolutes such as, "We go with all of my plan or nothing" or "There's nothing in your suggestion that is workable." Often when we're in the midst of a disagreement, it's helpful to simply state the facts: "It's reasonable that we would have different priorities on this."

In our example, Anthony's goal was to resolve Estelle's immediate problem and still get the rest of his work done for his other clients. After all, Estelle was an important client and his job was to be helpful, so he definitely wanted to avoid an argument. He decided to brainstorm possible ideas for an interim solution until the printer part could arrive.

 *T*ake one positive action.

Anthony called Estelle and said, "Estelle, I'm sorry that your printer isn't working. I know it's frustrating for you when it goes down and you hear all the complaints. I assure you that I'm working to get it fixed as soon as possible. Please tell me what happened." And then he calmly listened as Estelle vented (loudly). He remained emotionally detached and objectively summarized the facts of the situation for her. They worked together to figure out where in the company they could pull a "loaner" printer from, and he agreed to get to her office as soon as possible to switch out the printers and diagnose the problem with the broken printer.

Because Estelle is Anthony's customer, the Solution*SHIFT* is slanted in her direction. He should be flexible and accommodating, even though he has a contract that supports next-day repairs. If this had been an issue with a coworker, Anthony might have had a more open discussion. Perhaps he would have asked a teammate to be more flexible since they work together toward the same goals in the same company. See the difference?

Anthony recognized that it was in his best interest to let go of being right about the details of the service contract. He knew that when looking for solutions, **sometimes the strongest thing to do is to**

bend a little. As long as he stayed true to himself and his objective, he was in a good position to find the best solution for the situation. Anthony's boss complimented him on keeping his cool and resolving the problem for a key account, and Estelle was a happy customer despite all her huffing and puffing. WOW!

The next time you're hit with a problem POW, which will you choose – a solution stall or a Solution*SHIFT*?

*Being open minded and embracing a coworker's suggestion…**WOW!***

*Giving up the emotional fight for your solution…**WOW!***

*Finding a way to solve a client problem that works well for both of you…**WOW!***

SolutionSHIFT Exercise

This is your chance to apply what you've learned and a valuable step in creating a *SHIFT* habit. You may be thinking, "I don't want to do this exercise," but I assure you that practicing and personalizing the steps are crucial to making them work for you! (To download a free 8.5" x 11" version of this exercise, go to www.ProfessionalParadise.com.)

1. Under "POW," give a brief description of a recent problem, disagreement or conflict you had with a coworker or customer where there was a difference of opinion about next steps or possible solutions. Be sure to include your idea/solution and the other person's idea/solution.
2. Under "S," write the word STOP. (This will help you remember to say "Stop!" and breathe the next time you're hit with a POW.)
3. Under "H," list the harmful knee-jerk reactions you had in response to the POW you described in Step 1.
4. Under "I," list the negative emotions you experienced.
5. Under "F," list as many ideas as you can think of that are new options for the scenario you described.
6. Under "T," write down at least one action you will take if you are faced with this POW again.
7. Under "WOW," list the positive outcomes that would result from this Solution*SHIFT*.

POW	Stop and breathe	Harness knee-jerk reactions	Identify & manage negative emotions	Find new options	Take one positive action	WOW

PART III

GRAB YOUR PASSPORT AND GO!

Destination: Paradise

Lead your organization to Professional Paradise

When traveling abroad, a passport is the legal document which allows you to enter other countries. Your Passport to Professional Paradise represents the knowledge and skills you need to travel to your own version of Paradise, and it is now stamped with specific, proven strategies and techniques to *SHIFT* your POWs to WOWs. You can immediately put your Passport to use and be on your way...*if* that is your wish.

Some people are content in Prison or on Parole. They'd simply rather stay stuck in their comfort zone. Could that be you? If you want to get to Professional Paradise, you must first decide that you want to be there. There's a Volkswagen ad that says, "Misery has enough company...dare to be happy!" I wholeheartedly agree.

Most of you, however, are probably quite unhappy in Prison or on Parole and are ready to get out of Dodge. You know you want less stress, more energy and remarkable results at work. Good for you!

Making a conscious decision to *SHIFT* to Professional Paradise is critical to your success. Stephen Covey says, "Start with the end in mind." In Part I, you took the time to develop your vision of Professional Paradise. Now, create a Paradise Vision Card by taking that description and re-writing it on a piece of paper or typing it on the computer. (Or you can download a free Paradise Vision Card from www.ProfessionalParadise.com.) My vision card looks like this:

My Professional Paradise

I see people laughing and people who "get it."

I hear interesting dialogue and discussion about the topic at hand.

I think, "I'm so blessed to get to do this every day."

I say, "How can I be of service?"

I feel positive emotions – hope, joy, contentment, enthusiasm.

I am learning, creating new ideas, connecting people
and serving others.

I am paid fairly for my services.

I connect with like-minded people who sparkle and shine with
enthusiasm, *and* with people who need a "shot in the arm"
to get themselves back on track.

**My Professional Paradise is helping people escape from
Professional Prison and find their way to Professional Paradise.**

Once complete, take your vision card and post it in your office or work area. Attach it to the steering wheel or dashboard of your car. Put it someplace where you're sure to see it several times a day. Every time you look at it, take a minute or two to read it and envision it as if it is already happening.

With your Paradise destination constantly at the forefront of your mind, you will be more likely to remember to *SHIFT* your POWs to WOWs and to direct positive energy toward your goal. You'll begin to recognize the events, situations, interactions and circumstances that match your vision of Professional Paradise.

So how will you know when you've arrived in Paradise? Oh, you'll know, trust me.

More than likely, you'll notice the physical signs first. You'll find that you sleep better, have more energy, are far less stressed and experience better health. You might have fewer headaches and backaches. A healthy mindset supports a healthy body.

As your physical condition improves, so will your mental condition. Your concentration and ability to focus will get better. You'll find that you're more creative in general and more innovative in your problem solving. You'll spend more time "in the zone," so your assignments, projects and tasks will be easier to complete, and the workday will go by faster. And because you'll be creating positive connections with customers and coworkers, your communication and working relationships will improve.

All of these things bring about increased productivity which ultimately leads to remarkable results. And at the end of the day, isn't that what you really want – remarkable results, for you and for your organization? Remarkable results mean better performance reviews, which often translate into raises, bonuses and promotions. People who work in Professional Paradise often report that they have more financial success.

There are other, more subtle but just as important signs that you've arrived in Paradise. You'll be internally motivated to succeed. You'll be satisfied, fulfilled and have a sense of purpose. You might even catch yourself smiling or – heaven forbid – having fun! And of course, you'll discover the sense of happiness and bliss you've been looking for all along.

Oh yeah…and you'll actually enjoy going to work every day. What a concept!

I'll bet your family, loved ones and friends will notice when you arrive in Professional Paradise. They'll see the changes in you, possibly before you see them yourself.

Your customers (external and internal) will also notice. Paradise is contagious! When you are living the good life at work, your customers will be positively impacted by your work experience. Do you know who else will sit up and take notice when you reach your Paradise destination? Your colleagues, coworkers, boss and direct reports if you're a leader. The quality of *your* work life affects those you work with. You don't just create Professional Paradise for yourself, but also for your team, your department, even your entire organization. The number one reason to *SHIFT* to Professional Paradise is to benefit *you*. That's right – it's okay to put yourself first in this case. Why? Because you can't help others get to Paradise if you're not there yourself.

Every time I give a presentation at least one person asks, "Why do *I* always have to be the one to change?" or "Why do *I* have to change first?" I know some of you are thinking that same thing right now. And you may already know the answer deep down: because you're the only person you have control over and because you're the one who wants to work in Paradise.

Mahatma Gandhi said it best: "Be the change you want to see in the world." I think this is especially valuable wisdom in the workplace because we spend so much of our time working – more time, in fact, than just about anything else we do. So step up and become the model for others to follow. When you become the change you want to see and create your own Professional Paradise, you give others permission to do the same.

When you start to *SHIFT*, you'll notice a ripple effect that will be felt across your workplace. In his bestselling book *The Power of Intention*, Wayne Dyer shares research that just one person operating at a higher level of consciousness affects as many as *90,000 other people* who are stuck at a lower level. Talk about a ripple effect of the greatest magnitude!

Of course, you can't create Professional Paradise for someone else – that's an individual responsibility. But you can stay in Paradise yourself and be a delight to work with. Through your mindset and your actions, you can enhance the quality of work life others experience when they interact with you. Your ability to change your viewpoint, foster positive connections and find productive solutions contributes to your Professional Paradise as well as theirs. When *you* SHIFT, you literally start an upward spiral of positive energy.

Imagine you and everyone around you working in Professional Paradise each day. Just think about the amazing environment and the spectacular results that would ensue. It would indeed be Shangri-La.

One person has the power to start the groundswell for *SHIFT*ing to Professional Paradise. Why not be that person? You can be the rock that causes the ripple in your work pond and beyond. This is your chance to be a leader – regardless of your position in the organization.

Go ahead…lead your organization to Paradise and beyond!

Work, Sweet Work!

~~~~~~~~~~~~~~~~~~~~~~~~~

Set up permanent residence in Paradise

Just for a moment, think about how you feel on the last day – or maybe even the second-to-last day – of vacation. If you're like me, you get a knot in your stomach or maybe a lump in your throat. You enjoy the day, but you also start to dwell on the inevitable return to reality.

Wouldn't it be great if you didn't have to go back? Wouldn't you love to stay forever?

Unfortunately, an everlasting vacation isn't very likely. But you can set up permanent residence in Professional Paradise – your very own "Work, Sweet Work!" **You can make Professional Paradise your reality every day, day in and day out.** How?

First, **become the Chief Paradise Officer of your life.** In a nutshell, that means accepting total responsibility for the quality of your work experience and your professional life. No blaming the customer or the boss or the teammate in the next cubicle. Never forget that it is you who is in control. You have the power to imprison yourself or to set yourself free. Being the chief officer of anything involves responsibility, but it also offers great rewards. So hire yourself and get busy!

Second, **periodically re-evaluate your vision of Professional Paradise.** Do you remember the story I told at the beginning of the book about my job as a sales trainer and how it was Professional Paradise because I enjoyed the travel? Do you also remember how much that same job would have been Prison to me just a few years later when I was married with two children?

Our needs, wants, desires, likes, dislikes, goals and priorities change over time. As a result, how we define and describe Professional Paradise will change over time as well. If you don't stop every so often and reassess your vision of Paradise, you may find yourself locked up in Professional Prison. It's also a good idea to consider from time to time where you are on the Prison-Paradise Continuum. In our chaotic, busy world, it's easy to fall into the trap of living and working in survival mode – doing just enough to get by and get through each day. Before you know it, a year or two passes, and you look up one day to discover that you've been stuck on extended Parole.

The great news about Professional Paradise is that it's adaptable, flexible, changeable. It can be anything you want it to be – whatever suits you at any point in time. It won't look and feel the same throughout your entire career. As much as I enjoyed my work at the hospital, when I started my own business I found a different version of Professional Paradise – the next evolution of Paradise, if you will.

Right now, go put a reminder in your PDA or calendar to re-evaluate your situation at least once a year. Then go to www.ProfessionalParadise.com and download a free Paradise Vision

Card and Prison-Paradise Continuum and also put them in your PDA or calendar. When the time comes, re-do both exercises and see where you are. Remember, as long as you continue to re-evaluate, redefine and re-envision – and as long as you keep *SHIFT*ing – you will always have a place in Professional Paradise.

The third step to ensuring a permanent spot in Paradise is to **create a habit of *SHIFT*ing every POW to a WOW**. Without question, you will benefit from the first moment you try the *SHIFT* techniques and strategies. But to create lasting change you must develop a habit. If you want to stay in Paradise indefinitely, you can't just *SHIFT* the occasional POW to a WOW. Nor can you *SHIFT* for several months and then revert back to your old ways. You must create a habit and *SHIFT* to WOW every day.

Your brain works in amazing ways to form a habit. Think back to the time when you didn't know how to use a computer – before it became a habit. As you learned the steps and functions and keystrokes, you metaphorically cleared a path in your brain for how to navigate the computer and its software. Over time, as you repeated the steps, functions and keystrokes, you created a "rut" in your brain which holds the computer habit. Now, that rut is so deep and so worn, you can boot your computer and check email while talking on the phone and drinking a cup of coffee. Sound familiar?

This hardwiring of the brain is the reason habits are so hard to change. The habit ruts tend to persist, and the deeper they are (metaphorically speaking), the more difficult it is to eliminate them. The longer you've had a habit and the more often you use it, the harder it is to change. This is why stopping a habit is usually always harder than starting one. Think about it: Stop eating desserts or start making healthy dessert choices – which is easier? Stop getting annoyed or start being more patient? The "starting" seems more appealing – not to mention more doable – than the "stopping."

And so it is with POWs and WOWs. Which is easier – to stop your habitual responses to POWs or to start transforming your POWs into WOWs? *SHIFT* is not about stopping old habits as much as creating new, more positive habits. With practice – and distance from old habits – you will see great results and start to live the good life at work.

Stephen Covey, in *The 7 Habits of Highly Effective People*, shares that there are three elements to every habit: knowledge, skills and desire. When these three pieces converge and you do the necessary work, you are on your way toward developing a new habit. Forming a habit of *SHIFT*ing all your POWs to WOWs involves the same three elements:

1. **Knowledge – understanding how your work beliefs and your mindset affect your actions and outcomes.** The knowledge you've gained in this book about getting to Professional Paradise is deeply rooted in changing your beliefs and your thoughts to create new actions and outcomes. Clarify your descriptions of Prison, Parole and Paradise so you can recognize them. Acknowledge and decide to change any limiting work beliefs that are holding you back. Use your new knowledge to get out of Prison and get on with the journey.

2. **Skills – learning and executing the five *SHIFT* steps and applying the three *SHIFT* strategies in the workplace.** *SHIFT*ing a POW to a WOW is a skill which can only be honed through practice – lots of practice. Learning new skills isn't always easy and may "go against your grain" in the heat of the moment. Give yourself a pat on the back or a small

"Way to go!" inside your head each time you *SHIFT* a POW to a WOW. No more waiting for the boss or your customers to tell you how great you're doing – recognize yourself!

3. **Desire – consistently choosing to *SHIFT* because you want to live the good life at work.** If you consciously notice when you *SHIFT* a POW to a WOW, then you will enjoy the results and want to do it again. Make a concerted effort to monitor your thoughts and actions as they occur and decide if you like the outcomes. If you will just start using the *SHIFT* steps, I guarantee you'll see positive changes.

A Habit*SHIFT* (as I like to call it) typically takes 21 to 28 days according to the latest research. The best way to create a Habit*SHIFT* is to use your thoughts and actions to transform one POW at a time. Every day, for 28 days, use at least one *SHIFT* Strategy, and you'll form a new habit. It doesn't matter which strategy you use – you can use the same one each time or a different one. The steps, of course, are the same for all the strategies. Once you develop the habit of using the *SHIFT* steps, you'll do them automatically without thinking about which strategy you're using.

How can you keep the *SHIFT* steps and strategies on your radar while you form this new habit? One idea is to keep this book handy. When you feel a POW coming on, pull it out and review the *SHIFT* steps. Another option is to get a Passport to Professional Paradise memory card – a quick-reference card that lists the five *SHIFT* steps. Or you can utilize a *28-Day Diary*, the perfect tool for creating permanent *SHIFT* habits. (See page 125 or visit www.ProfessionalParadise.com for more details.)

Finally, if you want to stay in Professional Paradise long term, **pay attention to the care and feeding of your mind.** Your brain really does listen to all the messages you give it. Are you feeding it "food" that is nutritious or toxic? You need some Paradise Brain Food — and I don't mean fresh fish. What can you do for your mindset that will help you on your journey?

For starters, listen to the people around you. Listen to yourself for that matter. What do you say out loud and to yourself about work? You are in charge of your mindset. The images and ideas you put into your mind create the realities and experiences you live. "Garbage in, garbage out" works for your head just like it works in a computer processing system.

Who do you spend time with at work? Are you hanging out with the Chain Gang in your organization? Do you have lunch with people who are looking for WOWs or with the Dilbert® crowd? Choose your friends at work wisely. The more positive your peers are, the fewer POWs you will encounter.

Trust me when I tell you that once you get to Professional Paradise, you won't want to leave. In Paradise, every day is filled with sunshine and WOWs, and the workin' is fun and easy. Make a commitment to do what it takes to create your own Work, Sweet Work so you can live the good life indefinitely.

Paradise Found

Postcards from Paradise

All that you seek can be found right where you are.
— Abraham-Hicks Publications

You didn't seriously think I'd end this book without saying it one last time, did you? Professional Paradise — or Prison or Parole, for that matter — is not dependent on your job, your company, your boss, your coworkers or your customers. Do you see that now? Do you understand that the Professional Paradise you seek is right under your nose, just waiting for you to claim it?

When you picked up this book, you were likely either a doubter, a curious skeptic or a hopeful believer.

Which one are you now?

I hope you're a believer. I hope you know in your gut, your heart and your head that **Professional Paradise exists, you deserve it and you can get there.**

I'm fond of saying, "If you don't know the ending to a story, then why not write a happy one?" Write a happy ending to your work story. Decide to live happily ever after in Professional Paradise. You can do it — Professional Paradise is within your reach!

You have the key to release yourself from Prison. *Make a break…run for it!*

You have the knowledge and skills to get away from the limiting confines of Professional Parole. *SHIFT!*

You have the Passport that will get you all the way to your very own Professional Paradise. *Leave right now…today!*

And when you get there, kick off your shoes…put up the umbrella… lean back in that lounge chair…feel the breeze on your face…and dig your toes into the warm sand.

I ask only one thing as you live the good life at work — as you experience less stress, more energy and remarkable results…

Send me a "postcard."

Call me, email me (Vicki@VickHess.com) or visit me on the web and say just two words:

Paradise Found!

Acknowledgements

I now realize that "it takes a village" to write a book. Thank you to all the folks in my village who made the process so exciting and fulfilling.

My personal village is full of great men! To my husband, Alan, I love you just the way you are. Thanks for saying, "Go for it!" so often and then always being my biggest cheerleader. Josh…you are the calm in all storms. You inspire me to push a little harder and give a little more. Thanks for your thoughts and ideas along the way. Last but definitely not least, Brian…you work harder than anyone I know. Thanks for making sure my feet are always firmly planted on the ground.

Cindi and Kirk, Fran, Dan, Skip, Carol, Andrew, Warren, Kathy, Joy and Jeffrey — I so appreciate all your help along the way, and I value your friendship, support and assistance. Thanks also to many others who shared their opinions, suggestions and resources. There are simply too many of you to mention (here's a nod to "the Pod"), but rest assured that I know who you are and thank you for your contribution.

A note of gratitude goes to Juanell Teague and James Huggins who really got this ball rolling. Those two days I spent working with you were truly transformational in my journey to serve.

Thank you to Melissa Monogue of Back Porch Creative who brought vision and creativity to the cover and inside layout of the book. A big debt of gratitude goes out to David Cottrell, Principal of CornerStone Leadership Institute, for having faith in my work and for publishing/ distributing the book with me.

Thanks especially to Juli Baldwin, CEO of The Baldwin Group and chief book coach and editor, who helped me take this book to new levels that I never dreamed possible. You pushed and pulled in the gentlest of ways to extract the best I had to give. I've come to appreciate your wisdom, expertise, laughter, positive spirit and loving nature — thanks!

What Readers Have to Say ...

In a down to earth yet poignant style, Vicki is able to transport you from Prison to Professional Paradise in an easy hour read. This book offers real-life, practical skills that can be applied to both work-life and home-life. An easy read, this book shows that a little effort on the part of the reader will result in a great benefit for both the individual and those around him/her.

Neil M. Meltzer, "Escapee" and President
Sinai Hospital of Baltimore

SHIFT to Professional Paradise is a must read for everyone who wants to get control of their careers, maximize job satisfaction and improve performance while at the same time increasing their value to the business.

Jed B. Trosper, COO
GunnAllen Holding, Inc.

This book could not have come at a better time! My sales staff was entering into a new year filled with uncertainty, a tumbling economy, nothing but negativity on the nightly news...and me looking for creative ways to inspire sales when it appeared as if there were none to be had...Your book helped give my team new ways to tackle old problems and reminders to step back and think about what they really can control...I would recommend your book to anyone looking for a new way to present personal control over attitude and the positive impact on overall well-being.

Patty North, CPC, Regional Manager
Celebrity Staff, a division of C&A Industries

Hess has created an entertaining and practical resource for readers from all walks of life. The research sources are solid and the presentation is accessible to everyone. The SHIFT mnemonic is not just a clever memory tool, the associated steps and exercise can make a meaningful difference in the lives of those who choose to practice them. SHIFT is five more steps toward the fullest promise of life.

George "Skip" Casey, Ph.D.,
Assistant Vice President for Human Resources
Loyola University Maryland

In my work, I consistently find individuals who have sacrificed their ideal future for a life of mediocrity. Vicki has developed a simple and action-oriented message to help SHIFT us from a prison of scarcity to a paradise of abundance. Pick up this book, read it, and put it into action.

A. Paul Pyrz, Jr., President
LeaderShape, Inc.

About the Author

Vicki Hess, RN, MS, CSP is an *Escape Artist*. She helps people escape from Professional Prison and provides their passport to Professional Paradise. She is a highly-regarded professional in the field of employee engagement and workforce development. She brings hands on business and healthcare experience as well as substantial training expertise to her projects. In addition to over 25 years of professional experience, Vicki is a registered nurse and holds a masters degree from Towson University in Human Resource Development. Vicki worked in sales for Xerox Corporation, managed a training department at Entre' Computer Centers, and was responsible for team building, customer service and leadership development for LifeBridge Health, Inc. She provides motivating keynote presentations and is an expert on using her proprietary *SHIFT Strategies* to increase employee engagement. Her passion is using a shift in your viewpoint to create Professional Paradise for yourself, your coworkers, and your customers.

Vicki speaks locally and nationally on a variety of employee engagement related topics. In addition, Vicki was an adjunct professor in the graduate school of business at Johns Hopkins University. She is a professional member of the National Speakers Association (NSA). She is proud to be one of about 10% of speakers worldwide to have earned the Certified Speaking Professional (CSP) designation awarded by the NSA and the International Federation for Professional Speakers.

Vicki is also the author of *The Nurse Manager's Guide to Hiring, Firing & Inspiring* (Sigma Theta Tau International 2010). She publishes *Postcards from Professional Paradise* a free monthly e-newsletter and is a regular contributor to the Baltimore Business Journal and NurseTogether.com.

Vicki is happily married and the proud mother of two young men who are the source of most of her joy and much of her humor.

To learn more about how Vicki can lead you and your staff to Professional Paradise, please call 410-560-7212 or visit her website at www.**VickiHess**.com.

Vicki Hess – Escape Artist!
Popular Keynotes & Presentations

Vicki Hess, RN, MS, CSP, helps people escape from Professional Prison and provides their Passport to Professional Paradise where they experience less stress, more energy and increased productivity. In her category-of-one presentations, she uses proven business strategies plus music, storytelling and humor to create positive, long-term habit change even with the most skeptical audience members. Customizable keynotes and breakouts include:

SHIFT to Professional Paradise: Success Strategies for Living the Good Life at Work. This high-energy, engaging presentation will quickly dispel the notion that "work" is a four-letter word and show audience members how they can achieve remarkable results and fulfillment in their professional lives. Using the proprietary, proven, yet simple *SHIFT* methodology, participants will learn to turn POWs into WOWs and will walk away with the skills and tools necessary to create their own Professional Paradise.

Leading Your Organization to Professional Paradise and Beyond. Would employees say they work in Professional Prison or Professional Paradise? Evidence indicates that far too many people feel stuck in their jobs. Perhaps that's why disengagement is still consistently cited as a top concern within organizations. And while engagement is without question a personal matter, an organization's leadership plays a crucial role in supporting employees to create their own Professional Paradise. This presentation provides leaders with a proven methodology for creating an organization-wide culture of Professional Paradise.

Navigating the White Waters of Change: Will You Sink or *SHIFT?* Keeping up with the pace of organizational change can seem like an adventure on Class V rapids. What will happen the next time change impacts the workplace? Will people be able to enjoy the ride? Learn how to implement the proprietary *SHIFT* technique to maintain control, create energizing solutions and integrate change. Participants will jump aboard the raft and identify work beliefs and mindsets that affect their while they learn to use the *SHIFT* process to master the art of change management.

To book Vicki for your next meeting or conference, please call 410.560.7212. For more information about Vicki's other customized, creative keynotes and presentations, visit www.VickiHess.com.

More Ways to
SHIFT to Professional Paradise

1. Keynote Presentations

Let author Vicki Hess help your employees and leaders develop personal accountability for creating their own Professional Paradise and delivering remarkable business results. Vicki's high-energy, one-of-a-kind presentations are specifically designed to achieve long-term habit change for participants.

2. Professional Paradise Workshops and Web Workshops

Get everyone in your organization in Professional Paradise. Customized sessions focus on specific employee engagement challenges facing your employees and leaders. Web workshops offer the benefits of in-person training without the inconvenience and expense of travel.

3. Professional Paradise Resources

Powerful tools to help you practice and personalize the *SHIFT* steps and strategies.

+ *SHIFT* Exercise – *SHIFT* any POW to a WOW with this step-by-step guide
+ Prison-Paradise Continuum – where are you…Prison, Paradise or somewhere in between?
+ Paradise Vision Card – clarify and reinforce your personal vision of Professional Paradise
+ Passport to Professional Paradise Reminder Cards - quick-reference cards provide the *SHIFT* steps right at your fingertips

4. 28-Day Diary Series™

The perfect tool for creating permanent *SHIFT* habits, this set of innovative, pocket-size workbooks achieves long-term habit change in the areas of service, teamwork, communication and engagement.

Find FREE Downloadable Tools at www.**ProfessionalParadise**.com
410.560.7212

Find FREE Downloadable Tools at
www.ProfessionalParadise.com

To bring Vicki to your organization, visit
www.VickiHess.com

7004258R0

Made in the USA
Charleston, SC
09 January 2011